Buddhist Deities of Nepal:
Iconography in Two Sketchbooks

GUDRUN BÜHNEMANN

Buddhist Deities of Nepal: Iconography in Two Sketchbooks

Lumbini
2003

LUMBINI INTERNATIONAL RESEARCH INSTITUTE
OCCASIONAL PAPERS, 4

Lumbini International Research Institute
Occasional Papers, 4

Lumbini International Research Institute
P.O.Box 39
Bhairahawa, Dist. Rupandehi
NEPAL
e-mail: liri@mos.com.np

Cover: Nativity of the Buddha, 9th century, stone, h: 84 cm
Courtesy of the National Museum, Kathmandu

ISBN 99933-769-7-3

Published 2003
Printed in Nepal by Nepal Lithographing Co.

CONTENTS

1 Introduction

While I was examining microfilms of Tantric texts at the National Archives, Kathmandu, a film containing line drawings of Buddhist deities labelled 'Bauddha-devatācitrasaṃgraha' (= BDC) caught my attention. These drawings are similar to those in 'Nepalese Sketchbook no. 1' published by Lokesh Chandra (= LC) in 1984. Both sketchbooks, though apparently incomplete, contain a large number of drawings of deities. More extensive documents such as these are rarely found. I therefore decided to prepare a preliminary study of the sketchbooks since they comprise important documents for the field of Nevār Buddhist iconography.

Work on this project continued over a period of time. During my stay in Kathmandu in 2001 I first obtained a microfilm of the BDC from the National Archives and several weeks later a printed copy of the microfilm, on the basis of which I prepared a preliminary list of the deities' names. Later I had an opportunity to go over my reading of the names with Kāśīnāth Tamoṭ, which led to several improvements. After returning to the United States, I reworked my notes and modified and corrected my reading of the deities' names by consulting other iconographic source materials. I also began working on the LC. In an effort to obtain additional material for comparison, and hoping to find the original manuscript from which the BDC and LC were copied, I searched collections of sketchbooks in the U.S. But I have been unable to find the original sketchbook or similar sketchbooks. I also started correspondence with Dr. M. Blom, Utrecht, who kindly lent me several older microfilms containing material she obtained from the National Archives in the 1980s. While going through her films I found negatives of the BDC whose quality is superior to the microfilmed images I obtained from the National Archives. I therefore decided to use these negatives for reproduction of the sketchbook in this book, and I express my thanks to Dr. Blom for placing them at my disposal.

2 Previous Research on Sketchbooks

A large number of painters' sketchbooks or model books from Nepal are preserved in archives, museums and private collections in Nepal and the West. These sketchbooks contain drawings of deities, maṇḍalas, *mudrās* and related ritualistic objects for the use of craftsmen and painters. Very few have been published and studied. The artistic value of these materials varies greatly. Many sketchbooks are incomplete or damaged, others do not label their drawings and are therefore difficult to interpret. Blom 1985: 441 offers a brief classification of the extant types of sketchbooks. In her book 'Depicted Deities' (1989) she presents for the first time a contextual study of painters' model books and describes therein the characteristic features of these materials, their practical use and the importance of their study. In this valuable work, Blom focuses mostly on Hindu deities as depicted in Nepalese sketchbooks. Several scholars have studied individual sketchbooks pertaining to iconography. In the volume 'The Hindu Deities Illustrated according to the Pratiṣṭhālakṣaṇasāra-samuccaya' (1990), which I am currently revising for a South Asian edition, I analyze two Nepalese manuscripts which illustrate the deities described in Chapter 6 of the Pratiṣṭhālakṣaṇasārasamuccaya. Slightly more research has been done on Buddhist than on Hindu or Śaiva materials. Lowry 1977 provides a preliminary analysis of a Nepalese Buddhist sketchbook that differs stylistically from the sketchbooks reproduced in this book. Lokesh Chandra's volume 'Buddhist Iconography according to Nepalese Sketchbooks' (1984), which includes as an appendix a study of a Hindu sketchbook by A. Vergati, reproduces fragments of several Buddhist sketchbooks prefaced by a brief introduction. In a separate paper, Blom 1995 deals with the Buddhist Lokeśvara tradition in Nepal as reflected in painters' model books. Recently Slusser/Sharma/Giambrone 1999 studied a Nepalese sketchbook devoted to the metallurgical arts. A catalogue, titled 'The Circle of Bliss: Buddhist Meditational Art,' is currently being edited by J.C. Huntington and D. Bangdel to accompany an exhibition at the Los Angeles County Museum of Art in

October 2003. This forthcoming publication will include a study of a sketchbook by Chaya Chandrasekhar. This late-19th-century work (M 82.169.2 from the museum collection) depicts a large number of Buddhist and Śaiva deities, and is described in Pal 1985: 179 (D 28).

3 The Two Sketchbooks: The BDC and LC

This book reproduces two similar sets of line drawings of Buddhist deities. The first one, Bauddhadevatācitrasaṃgraha (= BDC), is hitherto unpublished. It is referred to in Blom 1989: 13–14, 84 and 1995: 140, 141, 143, 145, 147 (with reproductions of some drawings). The second sketchbook was published as 'Nepalese Sketchbook no. 1' by Lokesh Chandra (= LC) 1984: 1–19, but the drawings are rather dark and the details hard to distinguish. They are reproduced in this book in somewhat better quality and with a new list of deities' names. The BDC and LC appear to be copies of another sketchbook which has not yet been discovered.

3a The Sketchbook BDC

The first sketchbook, labelled 'Bauddhadevatācitrasaṃgraha (Rekhācitrātmaka),' consists of 186 drawings by one artist. It is preserved in the National Archives, Kathmandu only in microfilm (reel no. E 1866/2, running no. E 35548). The sketchbook was microfilmed by the staff of the Nepal-German Manuscript Preservation Project on October 10, 1985 from the private collection of a resident of Pāṭan whose surname is recorded as Harke [Harṣa]. During her stay in Kathmandu in the 1980s Blom was apparently able to see the original (see her brief description in Blom 1989: 14). The original sketchbook is no longer traceable, since it was returned to its owner after microfilming. The original document is recorded as a concertina-type manuscript (*thyāsaphū*) made of canvas and not – as usually is the case – paper. The size of the sketchbook is recorded as 25.6 x 17 cm, but on the microfilm which I obtained the drawings have been enlarged. Since the quality of the negatives obtained by M. Blom in the 1980s is superior to that of the microfilm copy supplied by the National Archives, the negatives were used for reproduction here. The sequence of pages in the negatives and the microfilm is identical, but may not be the original sequence of the drawings in the manuscript. It appears that some folios are out of sequence. The arrangement of deities is not very systematic and may not follow a particular text. The Lokeśvaras and some forms of Mañjuśrī, for example, are found in two different places. It is also possible that the sketchbook is incomplete. Since the pages are unnumbered and the original unavailable, I did not have enough evidence to justify rearranging the folios and have therefore retained the sequence in which the drawings were photographed. This sequence is as follows (an asterisk indicates that a folio may be out of sequence):

Folios	Deities
Folio 1*	Deities 1–5
Folio 2	Deities 6–8
Folio 3	Deities 9–11
Folio 4	Deities 12–15
Folio 5	Deities 16–20
Folio 6	Deities 21–24
Folio 7	Deities 25–28
Folio 8	Deities 29–33
Folio 9	Deities 34–37
Folio 10	Deities 38–42
Folio 11*	Deities 43–48
Folio 12	Deities 49–54

Folio 13	Deities 55–60
Folio 14	Deities 61–66
Folio 15*	Deities 67–73
Folio 16	Deities 74–79
Folio 17	Deities 80–85
Folio 18	Deities 86–93
Folio 19	Deities 94–99
Folio 20	Deities 100–107
Folio 21	Deities 108–115
Folio 22	Deities 116–123
Folio 23	Deities 124–130
Folio 24	Deities 131–136
Folio 25	Deities 137–142
Folio 26	Deities 143–148
Folio 27	Deities 149–154
Folio 28	Maṇḍala 155
Folio 29	Maṇḍala 156
Folio 30	Deities 157–162
Folio 31	Deities 163–168
Folio 32	Deities 169–174
Folio 33	Deities 175–180
Folio 34	Deities 181–186

Among the deities that figure prominently are the Lokeśvaras, forms of Mañjuśrī and Tārā. The manuscript also includes two maṇḍalas, which are not found in the LC. The first one is a maṇḍala of Cakrasaṃvara, which corresponds for the most part to the description in Abhayākaragupta's Niṣpannayogāvalī. The other is unnamed but can be identified as a maṇḍala of Mañjuśrī.

Most of the drawings are accompanied by the deities' names in Nevārī characters. The spellings of these names contain many errors. This is probably due to carelessness on the part of the scribe as well as lack of knowledge of Sanskrit. One also may note that in the orthography of Nevārī manuscripts long and short vowels are frequently interchanged, as are the letters *l*/*r*, *n*/*r*, *j*/*y*, *v*/*b*, *kh*/*ṣ* and *ś*/*ṣ*/*s*.[1] In listing the deities' names, I have standardized the orthography and corrected obvious scribal mistakes, for example, when the inscriptions substitute single for double consonants or dental for retroflex consonants. Thus I changed Mārici to Mārīcī,[2] Mahāvara to Mahābala and Vajrasatva to Vajrasattva. But I did not correct Nevārī variants of names, such as Vajradhāteśvarī[3] (for Vajradhātvīśvarī) or Halāhala (for Hālāhala). Other names are hybrid formations with Sanskrit, Prākr̥t and Nevārī elements. In such cases I have not attempted to make any changes either. The forms of names of Buddhist deities which are recorded as standard forms in reference works and dictionaries are often based on Bhattacharyya's edition of the Sādhanamālā and Niṣpannayogāvalī. In these editions Bhattacharyya has selected certain readings and rejected other local forms of names which are found in the manuscripts often enough to be considered local Nevārī variants. The names of the Lokeśvaras, which are based on local traditions, especially merit a detailed comparative study. Some readings of names are open to interpretation. In BDC 153, the inscription Kalpokta-Daśabhuja-Mārīcī (which seems to be the intended reading) can also be interpreted as (the equally possible compound) Karapātra-Daśabhuja-Mārīcī. In a few cases the names appear to be unusual and not attested elsewhere. Wherever a deity's name could not be determined with certainty I have discussed possible readings of the text in the footnotes. A final decision can only be made after comparing textual descriptions in

---

[1] For peculiarities in the orthography of Nevārī manuscripts, see Lienhard/Manandhar 1988: XXVII–XXVIII.

[2] I adopt the spelling Mārīcī recorded in the Monier-Williams 'Sanskrit-English Dictionary' and in Edgerton's 'Buddhist Hybrid Sanskrit Dictionary.' The reading Marīci is found in some manuscripts (Goshima/Noguchi 1983: 22, no. 81 and Hodgson 1874 [1972]: 19).

[3] The form Vajradhāteśvarī is also used in Williams/Tribe 2000: 211.

the *sādhana* collections related to Nepal with the drawings. At times I have found the names of deities to be inaccurate. In several cases names of attributes or hand gestures have been mistaken for a deity's name. In BDC 38, the word *tridaṇḍa*, referring to an attribute, is found instead of the name Prajñāpāramitā. In BDC 139 the word *dharmacakrasamādhi*, which refers to two *mudrā*s (i.e., *dharmacakramudrā* and *samādhimudrā*), appears instead of the name Mahāmantrānusāriṇī, one of the Pañcarakṣā goddesses. In another case (see below), a deity's name is derived from the colophon of a *sādhana* text. It is impossible to say whether the deities' names were added to the drawings by a later hand or not. Some drawings are not labelled at all; perhaps they were inserted later. Two of these unlabelled drawings can be identified as Lokeśvaras. Some deities may seem identical at first sight, but closer examination shows that different colours are specified for them. Other deities, such as the Pañcarakṣā goddesses, appear several times, each time following a different iconographic tradition. The deities' attributes are rarely labelled; if they are, Nevārī or Sanskrit words are used. At times an attribute is specified but not depicted in a drawing. On some folios, where attributes of deities were not clearly recognizable, a later hand redrew pairs of arms with attributes separately. It also appears that on some drawings the fingers of the hands of the deities have been redrawn.

I have assigned numbers to the drawings for easy reference. Table 1 summarizes the major iconographic characteristics of the deities: their names, number of arms and heads, postures and seats/mounts. In the table I have hyphenized long compounded names to help the reader unfamiliar with Sanskrit. Words in angle brackets indicate my additions. I have listed the number of heads of deities but not their colours. The BDC frequently specifies colours, but it is often unclear whether a colour refers to a deity's head or body. In the sketchbook the colours are indicated by the following abbreviations of Sanskrit and Nevārī (Nev.) words:

ku – for *kuni/kuvani* (Nev.) – smoke-coloured, or for *kuṅkuma* – saffron

te – *śveta* – white

va – *vāṅu* (Nev.) – green

ha – *harita* – green

ra – *rakta* – red

yū – for *yeyu* (Nev.) (?) – yellow

pi – *pīta* – yellow

ni – *nīla* – dark

I have only indicated the major postures: seated, standing, dancing and flying. Since the names of the postures are usually not specified in the sketchbook, it is not possible to distinguish, for example, between the standing postures *ālīḍha* and *pratyālīḍha*, which are defined differently by authorities. The column 'Seat/Mount' indicates the surface on which a deity is seated or standing. Such surfaces include animals, subjugated deities, lotuses, etc. The seats sometimes have several tiers. Among the subjugated deities on which a deity places a foot the group of four Māras (i.e., Brahmā, Viṣṇu/Nārāyaṇa, Mahādeva/Rudra and Indra) is specified several times. Several types of lotuses appear as seats of the deities. Some are double-petalled, others have petals pointing upwards or downwards. I have not included these details. The deities' attributes are not listed in the table, because many cannot be recognized clearly. Additional information such as cross-references to the deities' drawings in the LC can be found in the column 'Remarks.'

Kāśīnāth Tamoṭ places the BDC in the early 18th century based on linguistic evidence. This date agrees with Blom 1989: 14 and 1995: 140, who assigns the sketchbook to the 18th century.

3b The Sketchbook LC

The second sketchbook contains 171 drawings by a single artist who is not identical with the artist who prepared the line drawings in the BDC. It was first published by Lokesh Chandra (= LC) 1984: 1–19 as 'Nepalese Sketchbook no. 1' with very brief introductory remarks (introduction, p. 4). In his book, several folios are reproduced on a page with a single page number, and the deities' names are added at the bottom of a page. These names were apparently deciphered from the dark microfilmed or photographed copy of the drawings which is reproduced in the book and not from the original sketchbook. Already at that time, therefore, the inscriptions in the sketchbook were difficult to read: question marks were added to some names, while other deities remained unidentified. As Blom 1995: 140 already noted, the LC is very similar to the BDC. Comparing the LC with BDC enabled me to decipher some of the previously unidentified names and correct some readings of the names. However, some readings still remain tentative and can only be confirmed if the original becomes available. Lokesh Chandra informs me that the LC belonged to a Vajrācārya from Pāṭan.

For the reproduction of the LC in this book I have used a set of photocopies provided by Lokesh Chandra. I have maintained the arrangement of folios on the pages as followed in his book, but have assigned numbers to all the drawings (on the margins, from left to right) for easy reference. Table 2 summarizes the iconographic features of the deities following the same principles as in Table 1, but with cross references to the BDC. To avoid repetition, the notes on the iconographic features in Table 2 are less elaborate than those in Table 1. As Lokesh Chandra 1984: 4 already noted, and Mevissen 1998: 347–349 confirmed after examining the Pañcarakṣā images, the sequence of drawings in the LC is disordered. I have rearranged the folios only in so far as I have taken up the suggestion by Mevissen 1998: 349 that the second set of Pañcarakṣā images should precede the first set. This means that I have moved page 14 to the beginning of the collection and prefixed it to page 1 in Lokesh Chandra's 1984 edition. I did not have enough evidence to justify rearranging the order of other pages and have therefore retained their sequence. This sequence is as follows:

New arrangement	Arrangement in Lokesh Chandra 1984	Deities
Page 1	Page 14	Deities 1–9
Page 2	Page 1	Deities 10–15
Page 3	Page 2	Deities 16–23
Page 4	Page 3	Deities 24–31
Page 5	Page 4	Deities 32–39
Page 6	Page 5	Deities 40–47
Page 7	Page 6	Deities 48–57
Page 8	Page 7	Deities 58–68
Page 9	Page 8	Deities 69–79
Page 10	Page 9	Deities 80–89
Page 11	Page 10	Deities 90–100
Page 12	Page 11	Deities 101–110
Page 13	Page 12	Deities 111–119
Page 14	Page 13	Deities 120–124
Page 15	Page 15	Deities 125–133
Page 16	Page 16	Deities 134–144
Page 17	Page 17	Deities 145–155
Page 18	Page 18	Deities 156–166
Page 19	Page 19	Deities 167–171

3c Comparison of the BDC and LC

About two thirds of the 186 drawings in the BDC are very similar to the drawings in the LC. However, the last section of the drawings in the BDC (from 137 onwards) has no parallel in the LC. The sketchbook LC also contains several drawings not found in the BDC. In contrast to the BDC, the deities' attributes are frequently labelled in the LC. There are occasionally differences in the orthography of proper names between the two sketchbooks. In the drawing of one sketchbook the deity may be seated on a lotus, while the lotus may be absent in the drawing of the same deity in the other sketchbook. Occasionally the drawings contain errors. BDC 72 erroneously shows Ādibuddha-Mañjuśrī with nine arms, four on his right and five on his left side. Similarly, LC 81 depicts Amoghapāśa-Lokeśvara with seven arms. Both sketchbooks assign numbers to some of their line drawings. It appears as if the numbers were added later in the BDC after comparing the drawings with those in another document. The fact that the drawings in the BDC are not numbered in consecutive order and some numbers are entirely missing supports this assumption. The LC assigns numbers to only one of the two groups of Lokeśvaras, that is, the group of 32 Lokeśvaras. These same 32 Lokeśvaras appear also in the BDC, but with minor differences in the numbering. In the BDC the 32 Lokeśvaras are part of a larger group of 41 deities which includes forms of Prajñāpāramitā, Mañjuśrī and other deities.

One might wonder what practical purpose the sketchbooks served. Were their line drawings actually meant to be models for paintings or sculptures? This may well have been the case. From his study of the iconography of the Pañcarakṣā goddesses Mevissen 1998: 354 concludes that the artist of the line drawings in the LC made an effort to include iconographic types which were usually not depicted in Nepalese art by referring to descriptions in the *sādhana* collections and the Niṣpannayogāvalī. At least one deity's name in the LC and BDC can be shown to have been derived from the colophon of a *sādhana* text. The goddess in LC 166/BDC 99 is called 'Kiṃcid-vistara-Tārā.' This name can be traced back to Sādhanamālā[4] 98 whose colophon reads: *kiṃcidvistaraṃ tārāsādhanam*. The iconography of the goddess clearly corresponds to the description in Sādhanamālā 98, but in the body of the *sādhana* text the goddess is referred to as (Ārya)tārā.

4 Directions for Further Research

In his very brief introductory remarks to the LC (1984: 4), Lokesh Chandra traces the iconography of several deities to descriptions in the Sādhanamālā. For further study of the BDC and LC, collections of *sādhana*s related to Nepal are clearly the kinds of texts in which one should look for iconographic descriptions which correspond to the drawings. Among the deities whose iconography should be studied in detail are the Lokeśvaras.[5] Although useful materials on the Lokeśvara traditions in Nepal have become available in recent years, there is yet more scope for research.[6]

[4] As I have explained in Bühnemann 1994: 1–23, Bhattacharyya's 'Sādhanamālā' actually consists of *sādhana*s which the editoı compiled from several independent *sādhana* collections.

[5] The Lokeśvaras should not be referred to as Avalokiteśvaras. For the distinction between the Lokeśvaras and Avalokiteśvara, see Lokesh Chandra 1988: 29.

[6] Below I list some material on the Lokeśvaras which has come to my attention and may be useful to researchers. Deva 1984: 75–80 describes some forms of the Lokeśvaras popular in Nepal, and Blom 1995 discusses a number of problems related to the Nevār tradition. Lists of names of the Lokeśvaras according to Nepalese traditions have been published by several scholars. Bhattacharyya 1958: 394–431 provides descriptions and line drawings made of statues of 108 forms which were located at that time in Kathmandu's Machhendra Bāhā (also spelt Machhandar Vahal or Machhandra Bahal), also known as Jana Bāhā. He gives this section the misleading caption '108 Forms of Avalokiteśvara.' Locke 1980: 135–137 lists the names of the Lokeśvaras written below the wood carvings on the struts supporting the roof of the same temple. Lokesh Chandra 1981: 4 and 1984: 10–11 compares the names of the Lokeśvaras published by Bhattacharyya with those on line drawings made by three artists (Tantrikmuni Bajracharya, Ang Gelbu Sherpa and Gawang Tashi Sherpa, according to Lokesh Chandra 1981: 3 and 1984: 10). The artists prepared the drawings under Amoghabajra Bajracharya's supervision from paintings executed by Siddhimuni Sakya which have replaced the statues in the Bāhā. Lokesh Chandra also published a list of the names on Siddhimuni Sakya's paintings (1981: 16–18, 1984: 12–14) and the line drawings

In this book I present only a preliminary study of the two sketchbooks on the basis of the copies available to me. If the original sketchbooks or the original document from which both were most likely copied comes to light, problems regarding the reading of some of the deities' names and the sequence of drawings should easily be resolved. I hope that this small book will contribute to our knowledge of Nevār Buddhist iconography and will be useful to all who are interested in Buddhist iconography.

5 Acknowledgements

I thank Bishnu Kanta Sharma of the National Archives, Kathmandu, for permitting me to reproduce the BDC and Dr. M. Blom for making her negatives of the

---

based on his paintings (1981: 29–55, 1984: 341–367). In a special issue of the Journal Mikkyō Zuzō 8: 1990, Tachikawa/Hattori provide some information on the 108 Lokeśvaras in Jana Bāhā, followed by an essay on the paintings by Takaoka (in Japanese). This volume contains two sets of iconographic materials. The first set consists of contemporary line drawings of the 108 Lokeśvaras by Gautam Ratna Bajracharya, which were prepared on the basis of the paintings in Jana Bāhā (pp. 25–79). The second set consists of Takaoka's photographs of the paintings of the 108 Lokeśvaras in Jana Bāhā (pp. 81–135). It should be stated that in addition to the paintings of the 108 Lokeśvaras (which are preserved under glass), Jana Bāhā now also houses representations of the Lokeśvara group engraved on brass sheets. Lokesh Chandra presents a discussion (1981: 12–14, 1984: 14–16) and complete list of the names of the Lokeśvaras as found in a manuscript acquired by Raghu Vira (1981: 18–20, 1984: 11–12). In his detailed study of the thousand-armed Avalokiteśvara, Lokesh Chandra 1988: 38–42 lists the names of the Lokeśvaras according to additional sources. Gail specifies the names of 12 Lokeśvaras from Kvā Bāhā (1991: 40, plates XXXI–XXXIII) and of 24 Lokeśvaras from Caturbrahmamahāvihāra, Bhaktapur (1991: 48, plates XXXVI–XXXVIII). Blom 1996: 145 notes that a group of 38 Lokeśvaras is popular in Nepal and lists their names according to a sketchbook (1995: 147–148). While going through the manuscript collection of the National Archives, Kathmandu, I came across microfilm 5.267 (= Nepal German Manuscript Preservation Project, reel no. B 108/2) labelled 'Lokeśvaracitrabauddhamaṇḍalapratimā.' This most likely incomplete document consists of nine leaves with line drawings of the Lokeśvaras. The extant 27 Lokeśvara drawings are

sketchbook available to me. Dr. Lokesh Chandra graciously granted me permission to reproduce the LC and supplied me with a set of photocopies of the drawings. He not only encouraged me to publish the sketchbook again, but also helped in identifying some of the deities' names. I also acknowledge Kāśīnāth Tamoṭ's help in deciphering some of the names. I thank Dr. Charles E. Pain and Philip Pierce, M.A., for improving my English style. I owe thanks to the Lumbini International Research Institute and the University of Wisconsin-Madison for support during the different phases of my research. Finally I wish to thank Dr. Christoph Cüppers and the editorial board of the Lumbini International Research Institute for including this volume in their series.

Bibliography and Abbreviations

Amoghabajra Bajrācārya 1979. Nepāḥdeyā kanakacaityamahāvihārayā aṣṭottaraśata lokeśvarayā paricaya. <Kathmandu:> Lokeśvara Saṅgha (N.S. 1099).

BDC Bauddhadevatācitrasaṃgraha. 'Bauddhadevatācitrasaṃgraha (Rekhācitrātmaka),' microfilm preserved in the National Archives, Kathmandu (reel no. E 1866/2, running no. E 35548).

Bhattacharyya, B. 1958. The Indian Buddhist Iconography Mainly Based on the Sādhanamālā and Cognate Tāntric Texts of Rituals. Calcutta: Firma K.L. Mukhopadhyay (second edition, revised and enlarged).

Bhattacharyya, D.C. 1974. Tantric Buddhist Iconographic Sources. New Delhi: Munshiram Manoharlal Publishers Pvt. Ltd.

Bhattacharyya, D.C. 1978. Studies in Buddhist Iconography. New Delhi: Manohar Book Service.

Blom, M.L.B. 1985. Painters' Sketch-Books in Nepal with Special Reference to the Eight Mother-Goddesses in Bhaktapur. South Asian Archaeology: Papers from the Eighth International Conference of South Asian Archaeologists in Western Europe, held at Moesgaard Museum, Denmark, 1-5 July 1985. Edited by K. Frifelt and P. Sørensen. London: Curzon Press: 441–448.

Blom, M.L.B. 1989. Depicted Deities: Painters' Model Books in Nepal. Groningen: Egbert Forsten.

Blom, M. 1995. Lokeśvaras in Nepal. A living tradition? In: Function and Meaning in Buddhist Art. Proceedings of a seminar held at Leiden University 21–24 October 1991. Edited by K.R. van Kooij and H. van der Veere. Groningen: Egbert Forsten: 139–148.

Brinkhaus, H. 1985. Harihariharivāhana Lokeśvara in Nepal: Die Entwicklung einer Erscheinungsform Lokeśvaras vor dem Hintergrund religiöser Auseinandersetzung zwischen Buddhismus und Hinduismus in Nepal – dargestellt anhand literatur- und kunstgeschichtlicher Zeugnisse. Zeitschrift der Deutschen Morgenländischen Gesellschaft. Supplement 6. XXII. Deutscher Orientalistentag vom 21. bis 25. März 1983 in Tübingen. Ausgewählte Vorträge: 422–429.

Bühnemann, G. 1994. *Sādhanaśataka and *Sādhanaśatapañcāśikā. Two Buddhist Sādhana Collections in Sanskrit Manuscript. Vienna: Arbeitskreis für tibetische und buddhistische Studien.

Das Gupta, R. 1968. Nepalese Miniatures. Varanasi: Bharatiya Vidya Prakashan.

De Mallmann, M.-Th. 1948. Introduction à l'étude d'Avalokiteçvara. Paris: S.A.E.P.

De Mallmann, M.-Th. 1964. Étude iconographique sur Mañjuśrī. Paris: Maisonneuve.

De Mallmann, M.-Th. 1986. Introduction à l'iconographie du tântrisme bouddhique. Paris: Maisonneuve.

Deva, K. 1984. Images of Nepal. New Delhi: Archaeological Survey of India.

Dharmakośasaṃgraha. Dharmakośasaṃgraham <by Amr̥tānanda.> <Manuscript no. 8055 in the library of the Asiatic Society, Calcutta. Reproduced by Lokesh Chandra.> New Delhi: self-published (?) 1973. (For a description of this manuscript, written in 1826 A.D. upon the request of Brian Hodgson, cf. H.P. Shāstri: A Descriptive Catalogue of Sanscrit Manuscripts in the Government Collection under the Care of the Asiatic Society of Bengal. Volume I: Buddhist Manuscripts. Calcutta: Baptist Mission Press 1917: no. 119 [8055], pp. 191–193.)

Gail, A.J. 1991. Klöster in Nepal: Ikonographie buddhistischer Klöster im Kathmandutal. Graz: Akademische Druck- und Verlagsanstalt.

Goshima, K. and K. Noguchi 1983. A Succinct Catalogue of the Sanskrit Manuscripts in the Possession of the Faculty of Letters, Kyoto University. Kyoto: Kyoto University.

Gutschow, N. 1979. Der newarische Maler: Standortbestimmung in Gesellschaft, Raum und Ritus am Beispiel Bhaktapur/Nepal. Tribus (Veröffentlichungen des Linden-Museums) 28: 53–61.

Hodgson, B.H. 1874 (1972). Essays on the Languages, Literature and Religion of Nepal and Tibet Together with Further Papers on the Geography, Ethnology and Commerce of Those Countries. Corrected and Augmented Edition of Two Earlier Collections of Essays ... With a Supplement of Additions and Corrections From the Author's Copy. Edited by M.P. Saha And With Other Additions, Omitted in the Former Edition. Amsterdam: Philo Press.

Huntington, J.C./D. Bangdel 2003. The Circle of Bliss: Buddhist Meditational Art. Chicago: Arts Media Resources.
(This catalogue will accompany an exhibition at the Los Angeles County Museum of Art in October 2003 and is currently in preparation.)

Kölver, B. 1996. Constructing Pagodas according to Traditional Nepalese Drawings. Berlin: Akademie Verlag.

Kölver, U. and I. Shresthacarya 1994. A Dictionary of Contemporary Newari. Newari – English. Bonn: VGH Wissenschaftsverlag.

Kreijger, H.E. 1999. Kathmandu Valley Painting: The Jucker Collection. London: Serindia Publications.

LC Nepalese Sketchbook No. 1, published in Lokesh Chandra 1984: 1–19.

Lienhard/Manandhar 1988. Lienhard, S. with the collaboration of T.L. Manandhar. Nepalese Manuscripts. Part 1: Nevārī and Sanskrit, Staatsbibliothek preussischer Kulturbesitz, Berlin. Stuttgart: Franz Steiner Verlag.

Locke, J.K. 1980. Karunamaya: The Cult of Avalokitesvara–Matsyendranath In the Valley of Nepal. Kathmandu: Sahayogi Prakashan.

Locke, J.K. 1985. Buddhist Monasteries of Nepal: A Survey of the Bāhās and Bahīs of the Kathmandu Valley. Kathmandu: Sahayogi Press Pvt. Ltd.

Lokesh Chandra 1981. The 108 Forms of Lokeśvara in Hymns and Sculptures. New Delhi: International Academy of Indian Culture.

Lokesh Chandra 1984. Buddhist Iconography in Nepalese Sketch-Books. New Delhi: Jayyed Press.

Lokesh Chandra 1986. Buddhist Iconography of Tibet, begun by the late Prof. Raghu Vira. 2 volumes. Kyoto: Rinsen Book Company.

Lokesh Chandra 1988. The Thousand-Armed Avalokiteśvara. New Delhi: Abhinav Publications.

Lokesh Chandra 1999– . Dictionary of Buddhist Iconography. New Delhi: International Academy of Indian Culture and Aditya Prakashan.

Lowry, J. 1977. A Fifteenth Century Sketchbook (Preliminary Study). In: Essays sur l'art du Tibet. <Edited by> A. Macdonald, Y. Imaeda et al. Paris: Maisonneuve: 83–118.

Macdonald, A.W. and A.Vergati Stahl 1979. Newar Art: Nepalese Art during the Malla Period. Warminster: Aris & Phillips Ltd.

Manandhar, T.L. 1986. Newari–English Dictionary: Modern Language of Kathmandu Valley. By T.L. Manandhar, edited by A. Vergati. Delhi: Agam Kala Prakashan.

Mevissen, G.J.R. 1998. Deliberate Coincidence or Accidental Purpose? Pañcarakṣā Sequences in Xylographs and Sketchbooks. Berliner Indologische Studien 11/12: 307–364.

Mikkyō Zuzō 1990. This abbreviation is used for two sets of iconographic materials reproduced in the special issue of Mikkyō Zuzō (The Journal of Buddhist Iconography) 8: The 108 Lokeśvaras: Line Drawings by Gautam Ratna Bajracharya (pp. 25–79); The 108 Lokeśvaras at the Machhendra Nath Temple: Photographs by Hidenobu Takaoka (pp. 81–135).

Moser-Schmitt, E. 1983. Newar-Malerei aus Bhaktapur-Nepal. <Ausstellungskatalog.> Ausstellungsdauer: 24. April – 20. Mai 1983. Mannheim: Mannheimer Abendakademie.

Nev. Nevārī.

Niṣpannayogāvalī. Niṣpannayogāvalī of Mahāpaṇḍita Abhayākaragupta. Edited by B. Bhattacharyya. Baroda: Oriental Institute 1949.

Pal, P. 1974–1978. The Arts of Nepal. 2 parts. Leiden: E.J. Brill.

Pal, P. 1975. Nepal: Where the Gods are Young. New York: The Asia Society.

Pal, P. 1985. Art of Nepal. A Catalogue of the Los Angeles County Museum of Art Collection. Berkeley: Los Angeles County Museum of Art in association with University of California Press.

Pal, P. 1991. Art of the Himalayas: Treasures from Nepal and Tibet. New York: Hudson Hills Press.

Pal, P. 1993. Indian Painting: A Catalogue of the Los Angeles County Museum of Art Collection. Los Angeles: Los Angeles County Museum of Art.

Pratiṣṭhālakṣaṇasārasamuccaya. The Hindu Deities Illustrated according to the Pratiṣṭhālakṣaṇasārasamuccaya. Compiled by G. Bühnemann and M. Tachikawa. Tokyo: The Centre for East Asian Cultural Studies 1990.

Sādhanamālā. Edited by B. Bhattacharyya. 2 volumes. Baroda: Oriental Institute 1925–1928.

Sādhanamālā: Avalokiteśvara Section. Sanskrit and Tibetan. <Edited by> R. Sakuma. Delhi: Adroit Publishers 2002.

Shakya, Min B. 2000. Sacred Art of Nepal: Nepalese Paubha Paintings: Past and Present. Kathmandu: Handicraft Association of Nepal.

Slusser, M.S. 1982. Nepal Mandala: A Cultural Study of the Kathmandu Valley. 2 volumes. Princeton, New Jersey: Princeton University Press.

Slusser, M.S./N. Sharma/J.A. Giambrone 1999. Metamorphosis: Sheet Metal to Sacred Image in Nepal. Artibus Asiae 58: 215–232.

Tachikawa, M./S. Hattori 1990. The 108 Forms of Lokeśvara at the Machhendra Nath Temple. The Mikkyō Zuzō (The Journal of Buddhist Iconography) 8: 6–18 (in Japanese).

Takaoka, H. 1990. Remarks on the Paintings of the 108 Forms of Lokeśvara at the Machhendra Nath Temple. The Mikkyō Zuzō (The Journal of Buddhist Iconography) 8: 19–20 (in Japanese).

Van Kooij, K.R. 1977. The Iconography of the Buddhist Wood-carvings in a Newar Monastery in Kathmandu (Chuṣya-Bāhā). Journal of the Nepal Research Centre 1: 39–82.

Vergati, A. 1982. A Sketch-Book of Newar Iconography. Printed as an appendix in: Lokesh Chandra 1984: 1–59.

Williams, P./A. Tribe 2000. Buddhist Thought: A Complete Introduction to the Indian Tradition. London/New York: Routledge.

Table 1: The Iconographic Features of the Deities in the BDC

No.	Name	Arms	Heads	Posture	Seat/Mount	Remarks
1	Mañjuśrī	2	1	seated	lotus	cf. also 46; LC 56
2	Arapacana-Mañjuśrī	2	1	seated	lotus	cf. also 43; LC 55
3	< Arapacana->[1] Mañjuśrī (?)	2	1	seated	lotus	–
4	Vajrānaṅga-Mañjuśrī	6	1	standing	lotus	LC 58
5	Vajrānaṅga-Mañjuśrī	4	1	standing	lotus	LC 59
6	Ṣaḍakṣarī-Padmadhara	4	1	seated	lotus	LC 68
7	Siddhaikavīra-Mañjuśrī	2	1	seated	lotus	LC 61
8	Mahārājalīlā-Mañjuśrī[2]	2	1	seated	lion	LC 62
9	Nīlakaṇṭha-Lokeśvara	2	1	seated	snakes	LC 77
10	Unnamed	2	1	standing	–	–
11	Harihari<hari>vāhana-Lokeśvara[3]	6	1	seated	Hari riding Garuḍa who rides a lion	LC 73
12	Harihari<hari>vāhanod-bhava-Lokeśvara[4]	6	1	seated	Hari riding Garuḍa who rides a lion	LC 82
13	Vr̥dāyaka '5'	4	1	standing	lotus	LC 20
14	Śaṅkhanātha '6'	6	1	seated	Mahādeva riding a bull which is on a lotus	LC 21: Śaṅkharanātha

[1] The inscription is illegible.

[2] I.e., Mañjuśrī seated in the *mahārājalīlā* posture.

[3] The deity is labelled Hariharavāhano Lokeśvara.

[4] The inscription could also be interpreted as °vāhana-Avalokeśvara.

No.	Name	Arms	Heads	Posture	Seat/Mount	Remarks
15	Viṣṇukānta '7'	4	1	seated	Viṣṇu riding Garuḍa who is on a lotus	LC 23
16	Vajrahūtaka[5] '8'	16	1	dancing	lotus	LC 22
17	Kṛtāñjali '9'	12	1	standing	lotus	LC 24
18	Yamadaṇḍa '11'	4	1	standing	lotus	LC 26
19	Uṣṇīṣa '10'	10	1	standing	lotus	LC 25
20	Śāntaśrī (?)[6] '20'	6	1	standing	lotus	LC 27: Sāntāsi
21	Jñānadhātu '13'	6	1	seated	lotus	LC 28
22	Śākyabuddha (?)[7] '14'	6	1	seated	lotus	LC 29
23	Vajradhātu '15'	4	1	seated	lotus	LC 30
24	Mañjunātha '16'	6	1	seated	lotus	LC 31
25	Viśvahara[8] '17'	6	1	seated	lotus	LC 32
26	Dharmadhātu '18'	8	3	seated	horse on a lotus	LC 33
27	Amitābha '19'	6	1	seated	elephant on a lotus	LC 34
28	Mahāvajrasattva '20'	8	3	seated	lotus	LC 35
29	Siṃhanātha[9] '21'	6	1	seated	lotus	LC 36

[5] The name Vajrahuntika is found among the older representations of the 108 Lokeśvaras in Jana Bāhā; cf. Bhattacharyya 1958: 398, 409 (no. 35).

[6] The inscription reads 'Sānvāsi.' This Lokeśvara is found among the 108 Lokeśvaras in Jana Bāhā; cf. Bhattacharyya 1958: 397, no. 32 ('Sāntāsi') and Amoghabajra Bajrācārya 1979 and Mikkyō Zuzō 1990 (no. 77): Śāntaśrī. The LC also reads 'Sāntāsi.'

[7] The inscription can be read as 'Śāstṛbudha' or 'Śāstṛyudha.'

[8] Bhattacharyya 1958: 397 reads 'Viśvahana.'

[9] The deity Siṃhanātha differs from the iconographic type of Siṃhanāda (see also Gail 1991: 47).

No.	Name	Arms	Heads	Posture	Seat/Mount	Remarks
30	Unnamed	2	1	standing	snakes	–
31	Sahasrabhuja[10]	8	11	standing	–	LC 38
32	Sahasravajra '23'	8	11	standing	lotus	–
33	Dharmacakra '24'	10	3	seated	lotus	LC 39
34	Ṣaḍakṣarī '25'	4	1	seated	lotus	LC 40
35	Acāta '26'	6	1	seated	lotus	LC 41
36	Pupala-Mañjuśrī '31'	4	1	seated	lotus	LC 46: Pupala
37	Piṇḍapātra[11] '32'	4	1	seated	lotus	LC 47
38	'Tridaṇḍa'[12] <i.e., Prajñāpāramitā> '33'	6	1	seated	lotus	LC 48
39	Prajñāpāramitā '35'	2	1	seated	lotus	LC 51
40	Prajñāpāramitā '34'	4	1	seated	lotus	LC 49, 50
41	Prajñāpāramitā '36'	2	1	seated	lotus	LC 52
42	Halāhala[13] '22'	6 (?)	1	seated	–	with consort on left thigh; LC 37
43	Arapacana-Mañjuśrī '39'	2	1	seated	lotus	cf. also 2; LC 55
44	Prajñāpāramitā '37'	4	1	seated	lotus	LC 53
45	Prajñāpāramitā '38'	4	1	seated	lotus	LC 54
46	Mañjuśrī '40'	2	1	seated	lotus	cf. also 1; LC 56

[10] The numeral '23' was originally added to this drawing but later erased. This is an error, for '23' belongs here and not to the following line drawing.

[11] The inscription reads 'Piṇḍapāta.' This Lokeśvara is found among the 108 Lokeśvaras in Jana Bāhā; cf. Bhattacharyya 1958: 419, 428 (no. 73), Amoghabajra Bajrācārya 1979 and Mikkyō Zuzō 1990 (no. 36), who read Piṇḍapātra.

[12] The inscription reads 'Tiḍada.' The word *tridaṇḍa* seems to refer to the deity's attribute, not his name. LC 48 adds Prajñāpāramitā.

[13] Halāhala is a Nevārī variant of Hālāhala.

No.	Name	Arms	Heads	Posture	Seat/Mount	Remarks
47	Siddhaikavīra-Mañjuśrī ‘41’	2	1	seated	lotus	LC 57
48	Āryāvalokiteśvara[14] ‘4’	2	1	standing	–	LC 18
49	<Kamaṇḍalu-Lokeśvara ‘1’>[15]	6	1	standing	lotus	LC 16
50	Jñānadhātu ‘2’	6	1	standing	lotus	LC 17
51	Nṛtyanātha[16] ‘3’	10	1	dancing	lotus	LC 19
52	Lokanātha-Lokeśvara[17]	2	1	seated	lotus	LC 75
53	<Māyājālakrama-Krodha-Lokeśvara>[18]	12	5	standing	lotus	LC 78
54	Sugatisaṃdarśana-Lokeśvara	6	1	standing	lotus	LC 79
55	Amoghapāśa-Lokeśvara	8	1	standing	lotus	LC 84

[14] The inscription reads Ādyāvalokiteśvara.

[15] The drawing is unnamed. A similar Lokeśvara is found among the 108 Lokeśvaras in Jana Bāhā and is identified as Kamaṇḍalu-Lokeśvara; cf. Bhattacharyya 1958: 395, 403 (no. 10), Amoghabajra Bajrācārya 1979 and Mikkyō Zuzō 1990 (no. 99).

[16] The inscription reads ‘Nitenātha,’ a Nevārī variant of Sanskrit Nṛtyanātha. But the word *nite*/*nitye* also corresponds to Sanskrit *nitya* (Manandhar 1986: 129). Blom 1995 uses the spelling ‘Nītyanātha,’ which is found in some manuscripts in her article.

[17] The inscription reads: Lokanātha-Lalitākṣepa-Lokeśvara, i.e., Lokanātha-Lokeśvara in the *lalita* posture.

[18] The drawing is unnamed. A similar Lokeśvara is found among the 108 Lokeśvaras in Jana Bāhā and is identified as Māyājālakrama-Krodha-Lokeśvara; cf. Bhattacharyya 1958: 395, 403 (no. 15), Amoghabajra Bajrācārya 1979 and Mikkyō Zuzō 1990 (no. 94).

No.	Name	Arms	Heads	Posture	Seat/Mount	Remarks
56	Pretasaṃtarpita-Lokeśvara	6	1	standing	lotus?	with two Pretas; LC 80
57	Padmanr̥t<y>eśvara[19]	2	1	seated[20]	lotus	with consort on left thigh; LC 87
58	Gaṇapa	4	1	dancing	small mouse/shrew on a lotus	LC 89
59	Sukhāvatī-Lokeśvara	6	1	seated	lotus	LC 85
60	Mahākāla	2	1	standing	back of man	LC 92
61	Maitrī (= Maitreya[21])	4	3	seated	lotus	LC 93
62	Maitrī (= Maitreya)	2	1	seated	lotus	LC 94
63	Mahākāla	4	1	seated	men on a lotus	LC 91
64	Mahārāga-Mañjuśrī	8	4	seated	lotus	LC 90
65	Mañjuśrī	2	1	seated	lotus	LC 95
66	Mahākāla	2	1	standing	lotus	LC 96
67	Vajratīkṣṇa-Mañjuśrī[22]	2	1	seated	lotus	LC 97
68	Vajrakhaḍga-Mañjuśrī	2	1	seated	lotus	LC 98
69	Prajñājñāna-Mañjuśrī	2	1	seated	lotus	LC 99
70	Jñānakāya-Mañjuśrī	2	1	seated	lotus	LC 100
71	Vāgīśvara-Mañjuśrī	2	1	seated	lotus	LC 101

[19] Cf. LC 87 for the reading Padmanr̥tyeśvara; the inscription reads Paramanr̥teśvara. For the iconography of this deity, see Sādhanamālā 30. Bhattacharyya chooses the form Padmanarteśvara in his edition.

[20] The posture is specified as the comfortable posture (*sukhāsana*).

[21] Maitrī is a variant of Maitreya in Nepal.

[22] The inscription reads 'Vajrataki-Mañjuśrī.'

No.	Name	Arms	Heads	Posture	Seat/Mount	Remarks
72	Ādibuddha-Mañjuśrī	9 (!)[23]	5	seated	lotus	LC 102
73	Caturtha-Vajrāmr̥ta Amr̥takuṇḍalī[24]	6	3	standing	Gaṇapati	LC 106
74	Vajratīkṣṇa-Mañjuśrī[25]	8	4	standing	lotus	LC 104
75	Vajrajvālānalārka[26]	8	4	standing	Nārā<yaṇa>[27] and Lakṣmī	LC 108
76	Hayagrīva[28]	6	4	standing	lotus	top head is a horse's head; LC 110
77	Jambhala	2	1	dancing	lotus	LC 112
78	Yamāśvavajra[29]	8	4	standing	Indra, Indrāyaṇī, Lakṣmī, Jayakara, Siddhikara and Vasanta[30]	top head is a horse's head; four legs; LC 107

[23] The drawing shows four arms on the right side and (erroneously) five arms on the left side.

[24] The inscription reads 'Caturthavijayāsita-Amr̥takuṇḍalī.' This is the fourth (*caturtha*) Vajrāmr̥ta named Amr̥takuṇḍalī in a group of four; cf. the reference in Niṣpannayogāvalī p. 19, 11 with three other Vajrāmr̥ta deities in the Vajrāmr̥tatantra.

[25] The inscription reads 'Vajratrina-Mañjuśrī.'

[26] The inscription reads 'Vajrajvālānarka.'

[27] The LC reads Nārāyaṇa.

[28] The inscription reads Hayagiri.

[29] The deity is similar to Paramāśva (Niṣpannayogāvalī, p. 60, 7–12 and Sādhanamālā 261).

[30] The LC adds Madhukara to the list.

No.	Name	Arms	Heads	Posture	Seat/Mount	Remarks
79	Hayagrīva	2	2	standing	lotus	top head is a horse's head; LC 109
80	Hayagrīva	8	4	dancing	lotus	top head is a horse's head; LC 111
81	Ucchuṣma-Jambhala	2	1	standing	man	LC 113
82	Mahājambhala	6	3	seated	lotus	in union with consort; LC 114
83	Vasudhārā	2	1	seated	lotus	LC 115
84	Vasudhārā	2	1	seated	lotus	LC 116
85	Vasudhārā	6	1	seated	–	LC 127
86	Mahāsarasvatī	6	3	standing	lotus	LC 167
87	Vajraśāradā[31]	2	1	standing	lotus	LC 168
88	Vajrasarasvatī	2	1	seated	lotus	LC 169
89	Vajradhāteśvarī[32]	2	1	seated	lotus	LC 170
90	Pratyaṅgirā	6	1	seated	lotus	LC 171
91	Dhvajāgrakeyūra	4	4	standing	lotus	LC 118
92	Mahattarīpa-Tārā[33]	2	1	seated	lotus	LC 158

[31] The inscription reads Vajraśārakadā.

[32] The correct Sanskrit word is Vajradhātvīśvarī. The Nevārī variant Vajradhāteśvarī is also found in Williams/Tribe 2000: 211. For the interchangeability of the letters *ī* and *e* in the orthography of Nevārī manuscripts, see Lienhard/Manandhar 1988: XXVII.

[33] Probably for Mahattarī-Tārā, whose iconographic description is found in Sādhanamālā 90. The LC also reads Mahattarīpa-Tārā.

No.	Name	Arms	Heads	Posture	Seat/Mount	Remarks
93	Varada-Tārā	2	1	seated	lotus	LC 159
94	Aśoka-Tārā[34]	2	1	seated	lotus	with one attendant each right and left; LC 161
95	Sragdharā Tārā	2	1	standing	lotus	with one attendant each right and left; LC 157
96	Unnamed	2	1	seated	lotus	–
97	Bhadrāsana-Vaśyādhikāra-Tārā[35]	2	1	seated	lotus	LC 164
98	Vajratārā	8	3	seated	lotus	LC 165
99	'Kiṃcidvistara-Tārā'[36] (i.e., Āryatārā)	2	1	seated	lotus	LC 166
100	Viśvamātā	2	1	seated	elephant	LC 152
101	Prasanna-Tārā[37]	16	8	standing	four deities[38]	four legs; LC 153
102	Jāṅgulī Tārā	6	3	seated	–	LC 154
103	Jāṅgulī Tārā	4	1	seated	–	LC 155
104	Grahamātṛkā Tārā	6	3	seated	lotus	LC 134: Grahamātṛkā
105	Uṣṇīṣavijayā Tārā	8	3	seated	lotus	LC 135: Uṣṇīṣavijayā

[34] The inscription reads 'Aśvaku-Tārā.' For the interchangeability of the letters *o* and *va* in the orthography of Nevārī manuscripts, see Lienhard/Manandhar 1988: XXVII.

[35] I.e., Vaśyādhikāra-Tārā in the *bhadrāsana* posture (cf. Sādhanamālā 92).

[36] This name seems to be derived from the colophon of *sādhana* 98 in the Sādhanamālā, which specifies the *sādhana* as *kiṃcidvistaraṃ tārāsādhanam*. The central goddess of the *sādhana* is Āryatārā.

[37] The goddess is described in Sādhanamālā 114 with only two legs.

[38] The LC specifies them as Brahmā, Nārāyaṇa, Rudra and Indra. This group is known as the four Māras.

No.	Name	Arms	Heads	Posture	Seat/Mount	Remarks
106	Cundā Tārā	4	1	seated	–	LC 136
107	Parṇaśavarī Tārā	6	3	seated	lotus	LC 137
108	Parṇaśavarī Tārā	6	3	seated	lotus	LC 138
109	Prajñāpāramitā	2	1	seated	lotus	LC 139
110	Prajñāpāramitā	2	1	seated	lotus	LC 140
111	Prajñāpāramitā	4	1	seated	–	LC 141
112	Prajñāpāramitā	4	1	seated	–	LC 142
113	Bhr̥kuṭī Tārā[39]	4	1	standing	lotus	LC 143
114	Sitā<ta>patrā[40]	6	3	seated	lotus	LC 144
115	Dharmaśaṅkha- Dharmadhātu-Vāgīśvara[41]	2	1	seated	lotus	LC 125
116	Mahāvairocana	8	4	seated	–	LC 130
117	Mahāvairocana	2	4	seated	–	LC 133
118	Mahā-Amoghasiddhi	8	4	standing	lotus	LC 131
119	Mahāratnasaṃbhava *nāmasaṃgītisa lhāṅā* [42]	8	4	seated	–	LC 132
120	Dharmadhātu-Vāgīśvara	8	4	seated	lion	LC 128
121	Vajradhātu(samādhi)[43]	8	4	seated	lion	LC 129
122	Dharmadhātu-Vāgīśvara	8	3	seated	lotus	LC 126
123	Da<ṃ>va-Tārā[44]	2	1	standing	lotus	LC 127

[39] The inscription reads 'Bhr̥kuṭitī Tārā.'

[40] The inscription read °patra.

[41] The inscription reads Dharmaśaṅkhara-Dharmadhātu-Vāgīśvara.

[42] The addition *nāmasaṃgītisa lhāṅā* means 'mentioned in the Nāmasaṃgīti.'

[43] The deity's name is most likely Vajradhātu. The word *samādhi* may refer to the *samādhimudrā* displayed by two hands. Cf. 139 'Dharmacakrasamādhi.'

[44] The word *daṃva* means 'standing' in Nevārī.

No.	Name	Arms	Heads	Posture	Seat/Mount	Remarks
124	Pratisarā	10	3	seated	–	LC 2
125	Unnamed[45]	10	3	seated	lotus	in union with consort; LC 1
126	Sāhasrapramardanī	6	3	seated	lotus	LC 3
127	Māyūrī	2	1	seated	–	LC 4
128	Mantrānusāraṇī	4	1	seated	lotus	LC 5
129	Sitavatī	4	1	seated	lotus	LC 6
130	Pratisarā	8	4	seated	–	LC 7
131	Mahāmāyūrī	6	3	seated	–	LC 8
132	Sāhasrapramardanī	6	3	seated	lotus	LC 9
133	Sitavatī	4	3	seated	lotus	LC 10: Śītavatī
134	Mantrānusāraṇī	4	1	seated	–	LC 11
135	Mahāpratisarā	12	4	seated	–	LC 12 (three-headed)
136	Mahāsāhasrapramardanī	10	4	seated	men	LC 13
137	Mahāmāyūrī	8	3	seated	lotus	LC 14
138	Mahāsitavatī	8	3	seated	lotus	–
139	'Dharmacakrasamādhi' <i.e., Mahāmantrānusāraṇī>[46]	12	3	seated	–	–
140	Jñānaḍākinī	6	3	seated	lotus, but labelled *siṃhāsana*	–

[45] In LC 1 this unidentified deity is much larger than the Pañcarakṣā goddesses. This may suggest that the goddesses are considered subordinate to this deity.

[46] The inscription refers to the goddess as 'Dharmacakrasamādhi,' since she displays the *dharmacakra-mudrā* and *samādhimudrā*. The goddess can be identified as Mahāmantrānusāraṇī. For this iconographic type, see Mevissen 1998: 334–335.

No.	Name	Arms	Heads	Posture	Seat/Mount	Remarks
141	Vajratārā	8	4	seated	lotus	–
142	Bhūtaḍāmara/Ḍāmara[47]	4	1	standing	divine being[48]	–
143	Vajrapāṇi	2	1	standing	–	–
144	Mahābala	2	1	standing	–	–
145	Mahābala	4	1	standing	–	–
146	Vighnāntaka	8	1	standing	Gaṇapati	–
147	Vighnāntaka	6	1	standing	Gaṇapati	–
148	Vighnāntaka	2	1	standing	Gaṇapati	–
149	Aṣṭabhuja-Mārīcī	8	3	standing	five pigs	one head is a pig's head
150	Uḍḍiyāna-Mārīcī	12	6	standing	five pigs	one head is a pig's head
151	Uḍḍiyāna-Mārīcī	12	6?	standing	three pigs	–
152	Mārīcī	6	3	standing	three pigs	–
153	Kalpokta-Daśabhuja-Mārīcī[49]	10	5	standing	three pigs	–

[47] Both names are inscribed.

[48] Aparājita would be expected but no name is specified.

[49] Cf. Sādhanamālā 135, whose colophon states: Kalpoktasitamārīcīsādhana. One could also read the inscription as 'Karapātra-Daśabhuja-Mārīcī.'

No.	Name	Arms	Heads	Posture	Seat/Mount	Remarks
154	Aśokakānta-Mārīcī	2	1	seated	pig	–
155	Cakrasaṃvara	12	4	standing	two deities[50]	in a maṇḍala; in union with Vajravārāhī; surrounded by Khasūrohā (= Khaṇḍarohā), Lāmā, Ḍākinī, Rūpiṇī, Śvānāsyā, Yamadaṃṣṭrī, Ulūkāsyā, Yamamathanī, Kākāsyā, Yamadāḍhinī, Śūkarāsyā and Yamadūtī[51]
156	<Mañjuśrī>[52]	6	3	seated	lotus	in a maṇḍala, surrounded by the ten Krodhas

[50] Bhairava and Kālarātrī are expected, as in Niṣpannayogāvalī, maṇḍala 12.
[51] Cf. Niṣpannayogāvalī, maṇḍala 12 (Saṃvaramaṇḍala).
[52] The deity is unnamed. A similar iconographic form of Mañjuśrī seems to be featured on the wooden *toraṇa* of the main gate to Rato Macchendranath, Kathmandu. A contemporary *paubha* from Pāṭan, Nepal "usually displayed in the Hiranya Varna Mahavihara ("Golden Temple") during the Bahidyo Boyegu ceremony in the month of August every year" (Shakya 2000: 77) represents a similar iconographic type and is reproduced in Shakya 2000, plate 17. The *paubha* shows Mañjuśrī with three heads and six arms. His two main hands display the *dharmacakramudrā* while holding his *vajra* and bell. In his other hands, the deity holds a sword and manuscript placed on a lotus, and a final pair of attributes, the bow and arrow. The Mañjuśrī in the centre of our maṇḍala displays the *dharmacakramudrā* without the *vajra* and bell. The other attributes are identical, except that the manuscript is missing (only a lotus is shown).

No.	Name	Arms	Heads	Posture	Seat/Mount	Remarks
157	Acala	2	1	standing	Brahmā, Nārā<ya-ṇa>,[53] Mahādeva and Indra	–
158	Vidyujjvālākarālī nāmaikajaṭā-Tārā[54]	24	9 (?)[55]	standing	Brahmā, Viṣṇu, Mahādeva and Indra[56]	–
159	Ekajaṭā Tārā	4	1	standing	lotus	–
160	Ekajaṭā Tārā	8	1	standing	skull bowl	–
161	Ekajaṭā Tārā	2	1	flying?	skull bowl	–
162	Buddhakapāla	4	1	dancing	man	–
163	Vajraghoṇā	4	1	standing	man	having a pig's head
164	Ekajaṭā Tārā, *aṣṭabhujā*	8	1	standing	lotus	–
165	Ekajaṭā Tārā	2	1	standing	lotus	–
166	Ūrdhvapāda-Vajrayoginī	2	1	standing	Kālī and Bhairava	–
167	Vidyādharī <Vajrayoginī>	2	1	flying	Kālī and Bhairava	–
168	Vajrayogi<nī>	2	1	standing	Kālī and Bhairava	–

[53] For a Nepalese representation of Acala (with his consort Viśvavajrī), who places his feet on Brahmā, Śiva, Viṣṇu and Indra, see plate 19 in Kreijger 1999.

[54] In accordance with Sādhanamālā 123; the inscription reads 'Vidyujjvālākarāmukhaikajaṭātārā.'

[55] According to Sādhanamālā 123, the deity should have twelve heads.

[56] The names of the four Māras are inscribed but only two deities are depicted.

No.	Name	Arms	Heads	Posture	Seat/Mount	Remarks
169	Vajravārāhī	2	2	dancing	man	pig's face on right side of head
170	Vajravārāhī	2	1	dancing	man	–
171	Ādivajrayoginī	2	1	standing	meṇ	–
172	Yogāmbara	6	3	seated	lotus on lion	in union with consort
173	Śrī-Yogāmbara	6	3	seated	lotus on lion	in union with consort
174	Kr̥ṣṇayamāri	10	3	standing	bull	in union with consort
175	'Belonging to the <Guhya>samāja' (*samājayā*)[57]	10	3	seated	lotus	in union with consort
176	Mañjuvajra	10	3	seated	lotus	in union with consort
177	Dvibhuja-Hevajra	2	1	dancing	man	in union with consort
178	Sa<ṃpuṭa->ukta-(?)-Vajrasattva[58]	10	3	dancing	–	in union with consort

[57] The particle *-yā* denotes the genitive case in Nevārī, so that the form appearing here may mean 'of Guhyasamāja.' It is also used as an adjectival suffix meaning 'related to.' It would then refer to a deity of the Guhyasamāja such as Guhyasamāja-Akṣobhya or Guhyasamāja-Vajrasattva.

[58] I.e., Vajrasattva as described in the Saṃpuṭa(tantra)? The inscription reads 'Sakukta-Vajrasattva.' The iconography of the deity is similar to that of Vajrasattva as described in Niṣpannayogāvalī, p. 8, 17 – 22, but according to the description in the Niṣpannayogāvalī the deity should have six arms. In that text the maṇḍala is referred to as the 'Śrīsaṃpuṭatantroktavajrasattvamaṇḍala,' the 'Maṇḍala of Vajrasattva as described in the Saṃpuṭatantra.' One could also interpret the inscription as Ṣaḍbhuja-Vajrasattva, 'Six-armed Vajrasattva,' but the drawing shows (erroneously?) ten arms.

No.	Name	Arms	Heads	Posture	Seat/Mount	Remarks
179	Caturbhuja-Hevajra	4	3	dancing	man	in union with consort
180	Praharaṇamat-Hevajra[59]	16	8	seated and standing	Brahmā, Viṣṇu, <Mahā-deva>[60] and Indra	four legs; in union with consort
181	Ṣaḍbhuja-Hevajra	6	1	dancing	–	in union with consort
182	Dvibhuja-Hevajra	2	1	dancing	man	in union with consort
183	Hevajra-Kurukullā[61]	4	1	dancing	man?	–
184	Hevajra, *caturbhuja*	4	1	dancing	man	in union with consort
185	Unnamed	10	1	seated	lotus	in union with consort
186	Hevajra, *ṣaḍbhuja*	6	1	dancing	man	in union with consort

[59] Praharaṇamat-Hevajra ('Hevajra possessing weapons') is a type of Hevajra who is visualized as holding weapons and follows the tradition of the Saṃpuṭatantra. This form of Hevajra is described in Niṣpannayogāvalī, pp. 14, 20 – 15, 2; cf. also Lokesh Chandra 1999–, Volume 1, introduction, p. XLV. This form differs from Hevajra holding skull-bowls (Kapāladhara-Hevajra); for Kapāladhara-Hevajra, see Kreijger 1999, plate 31.

[60] Part of the inscription was cut off in the photograph.

[61] I.e., Hevajrakrama-Kurukullā. For this deity, see De Mallmann 1986: 228.

The Sketchbook B/DC

1 2 3

4 5

6 7 8

9 10 11

12 13

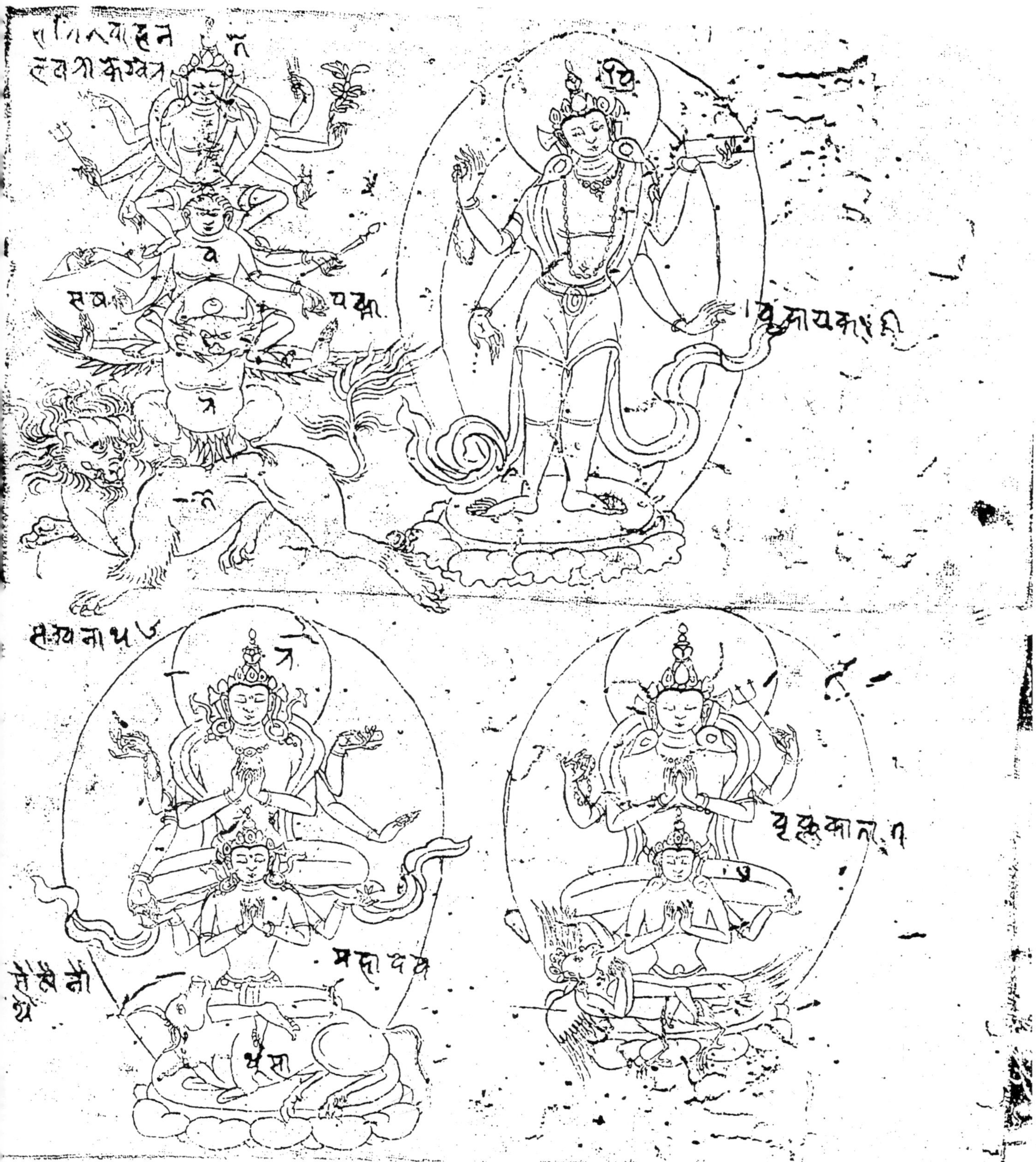

14 15

16 17

18 19 20

21 22

23 24

25 26

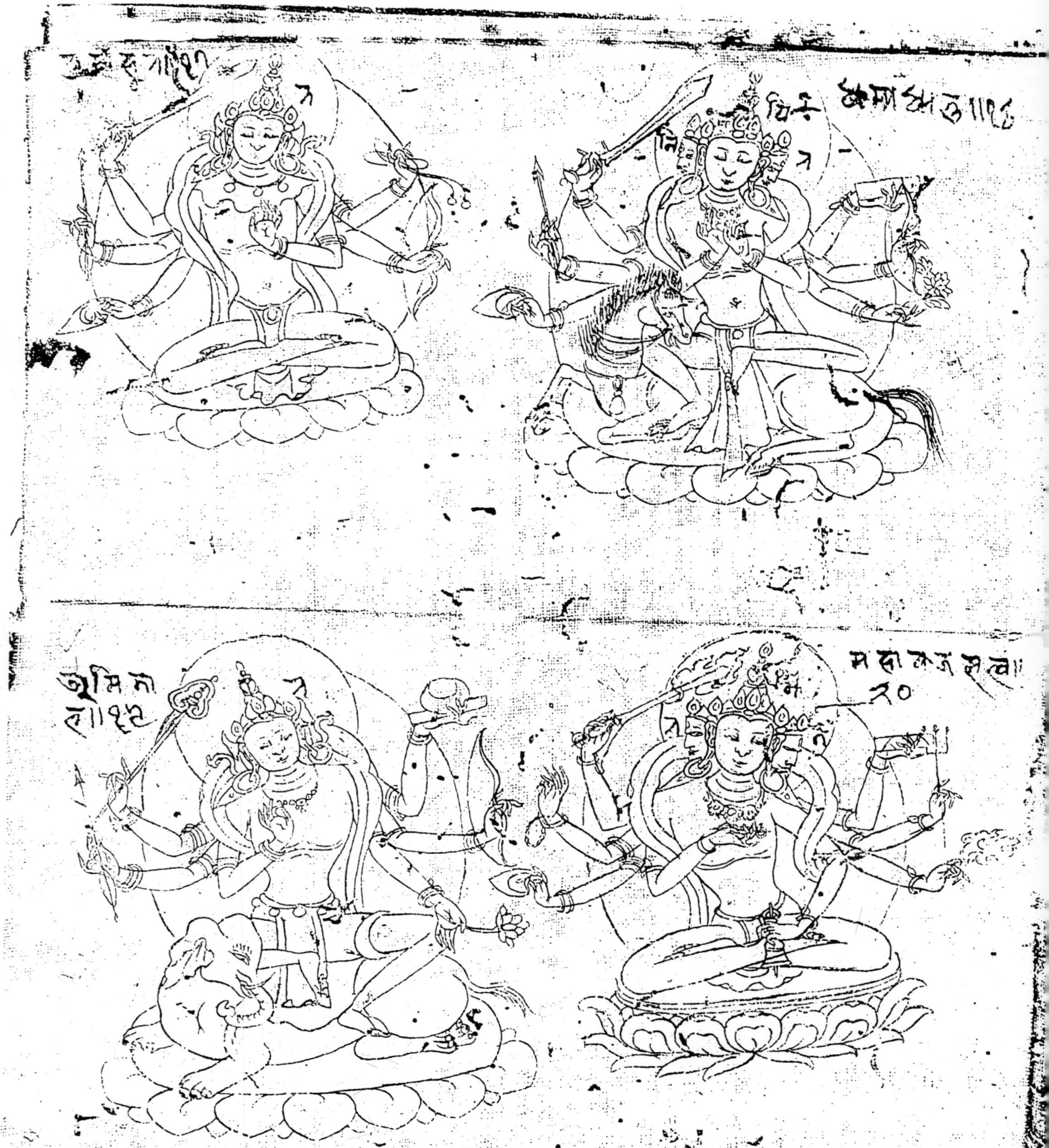

27 28

29 30 31

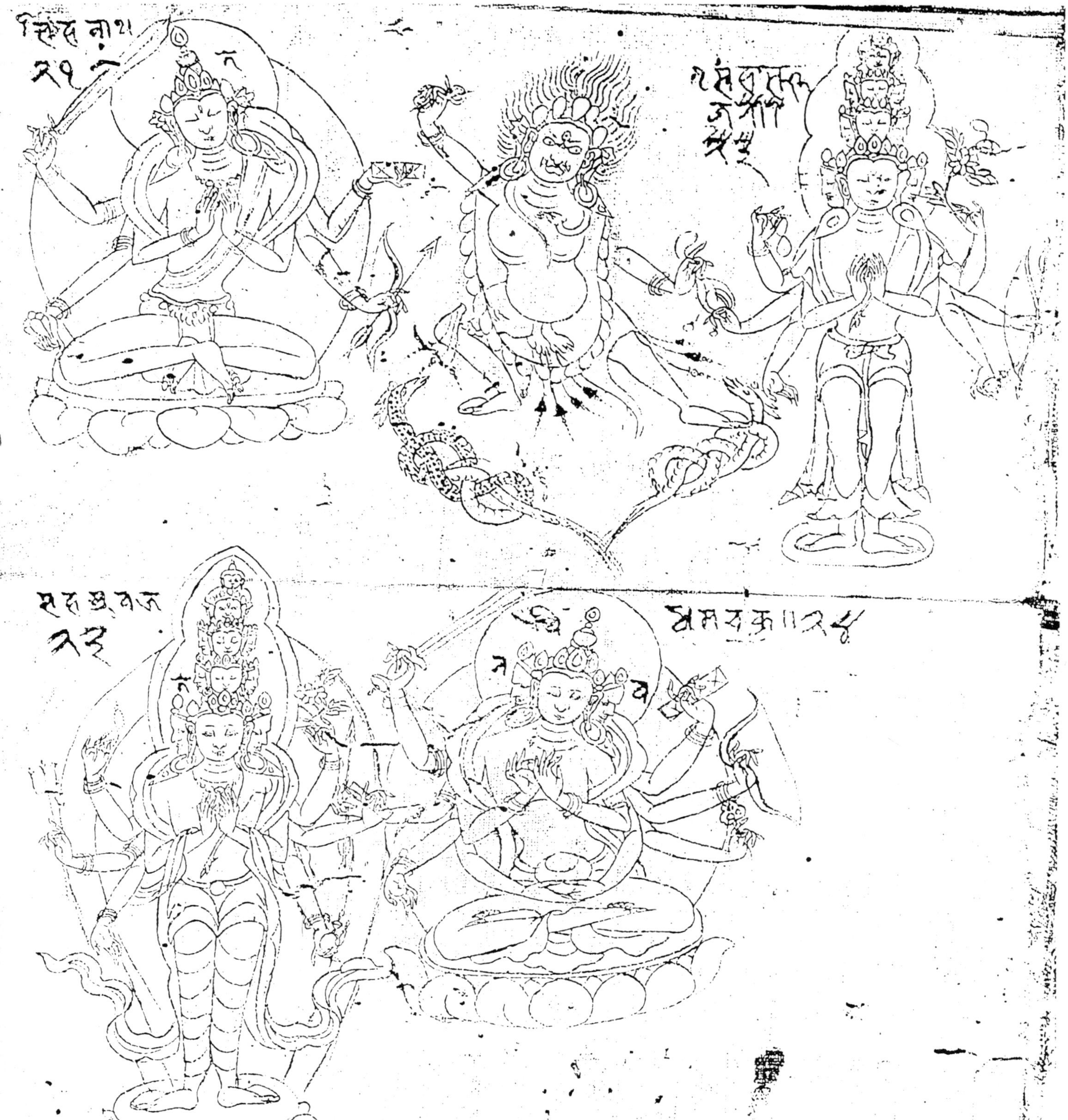

32 33

34 35

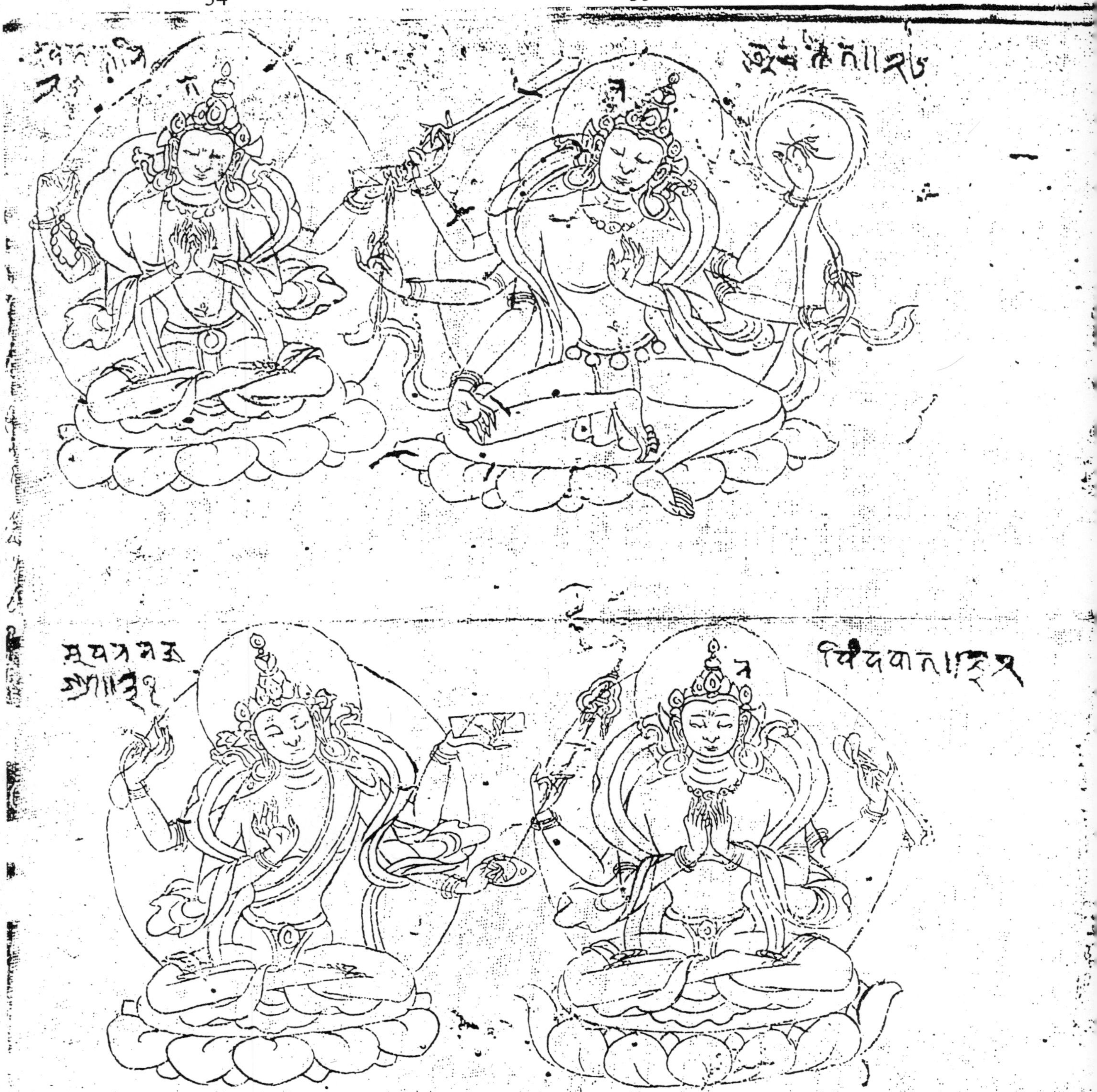

36 37

38 39

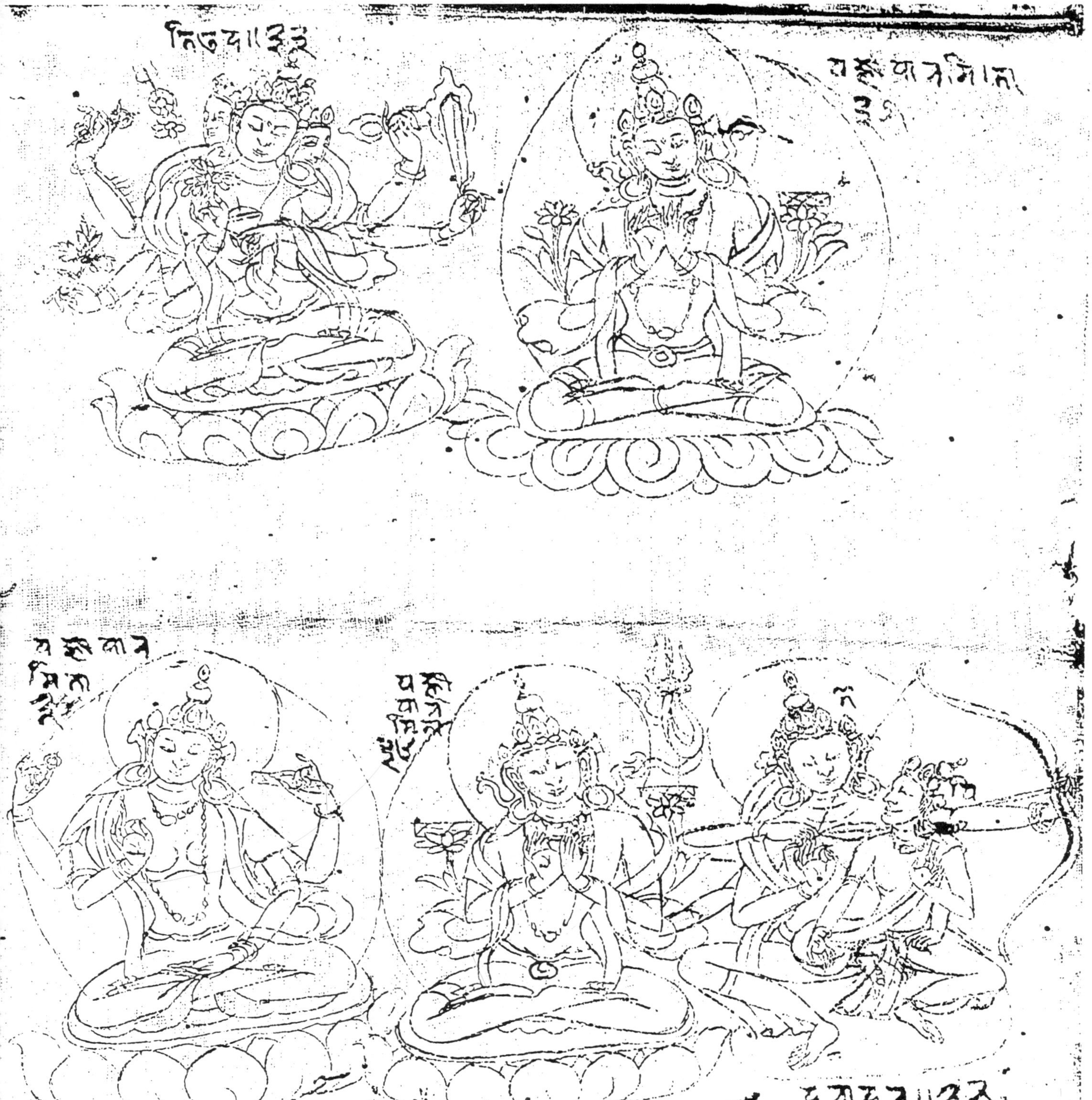

40 41 42

43 44 45

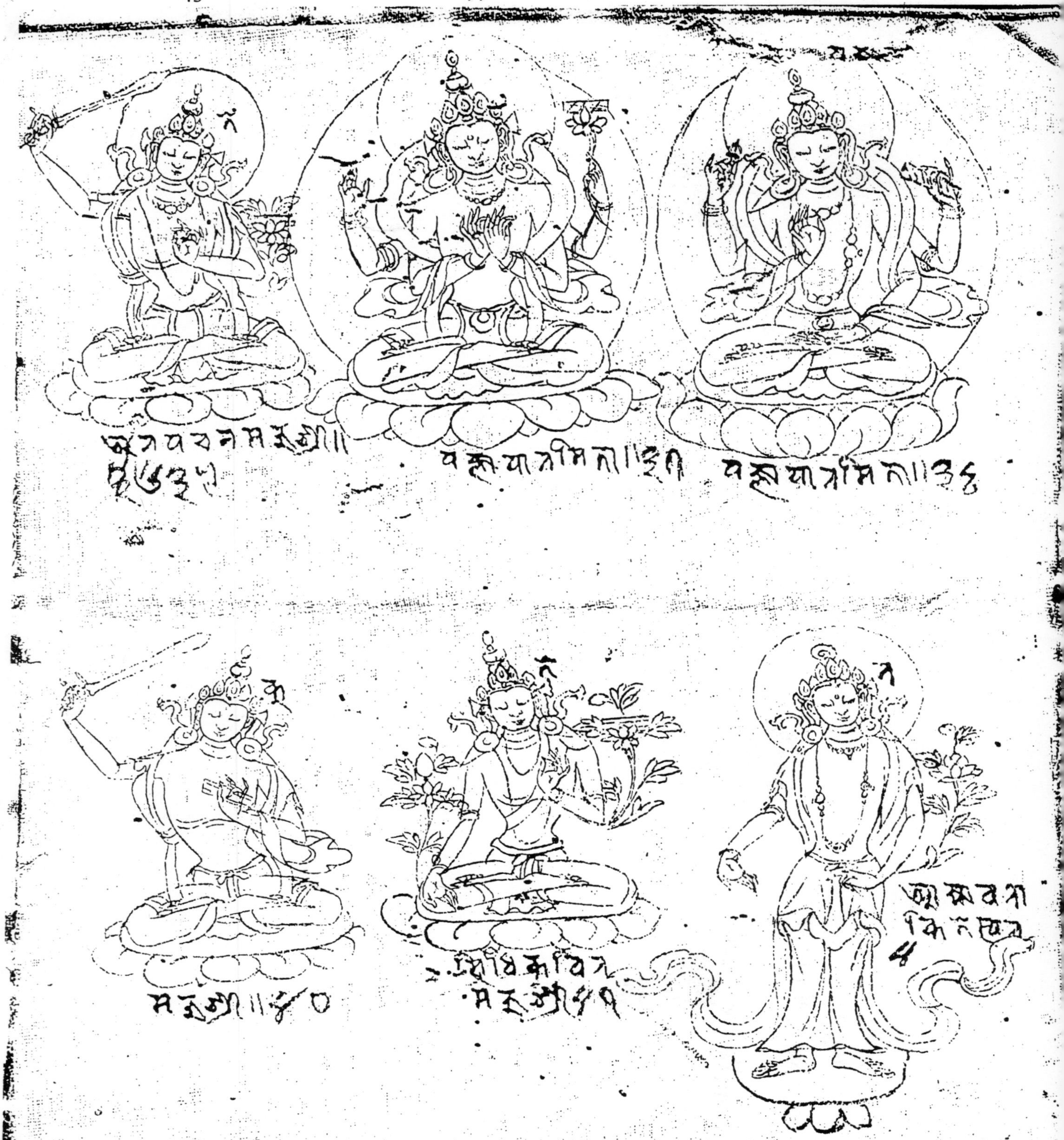

46 47 48

49 50 51

52 53 54

55 56 57

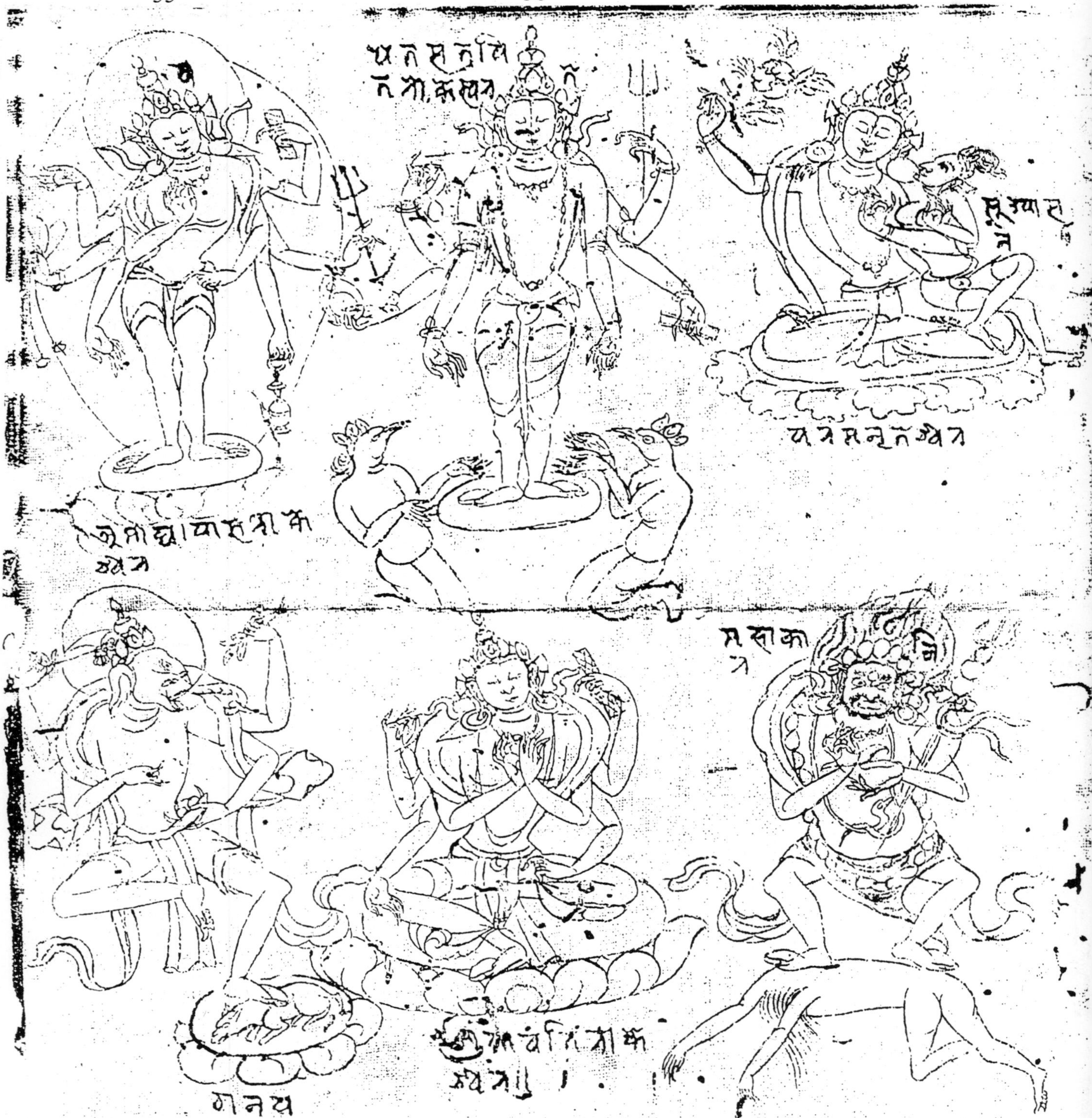

58 59 60

61

62

63

64

65

66

67 68 69 70

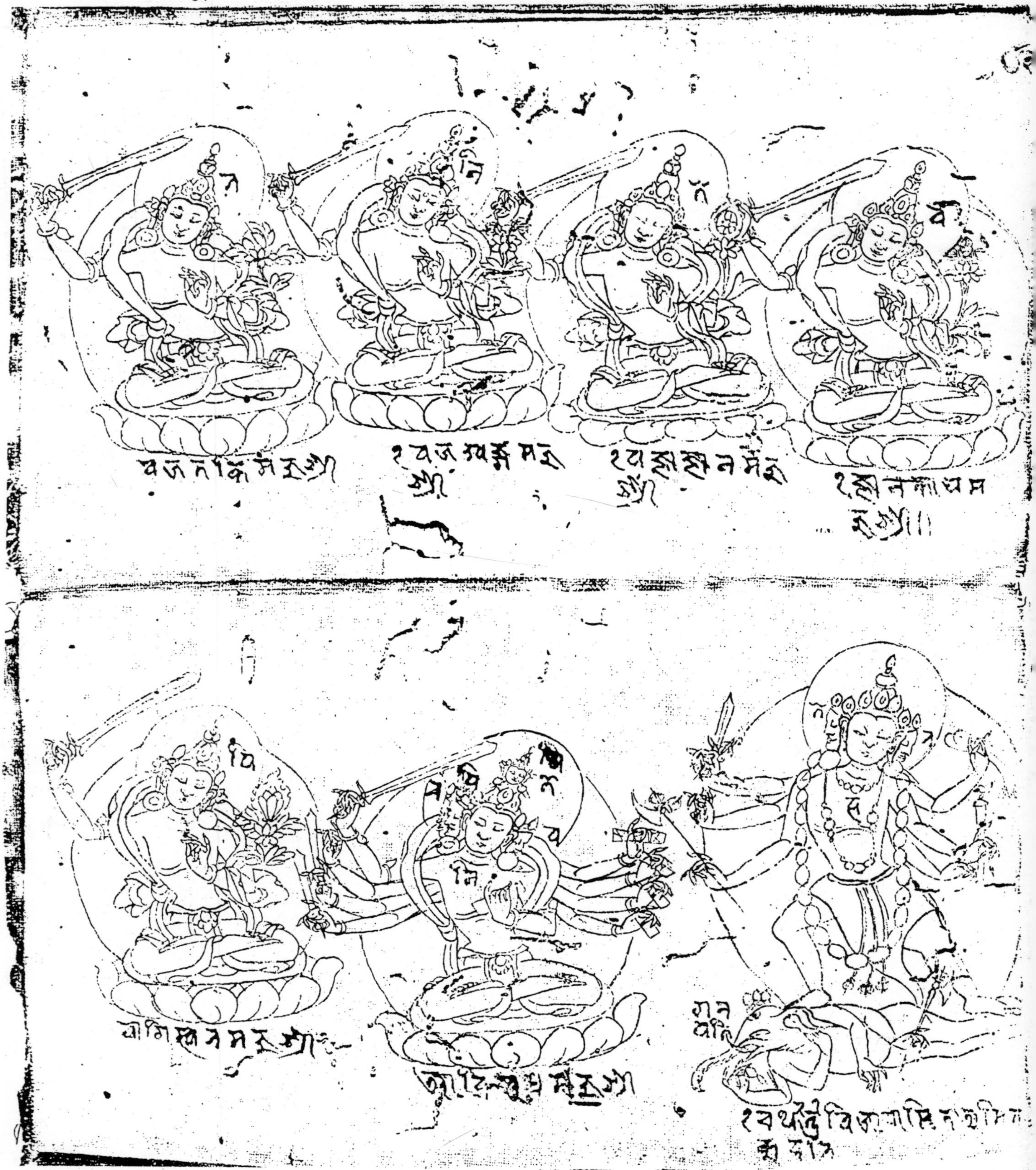

71 72 73

74 75 76

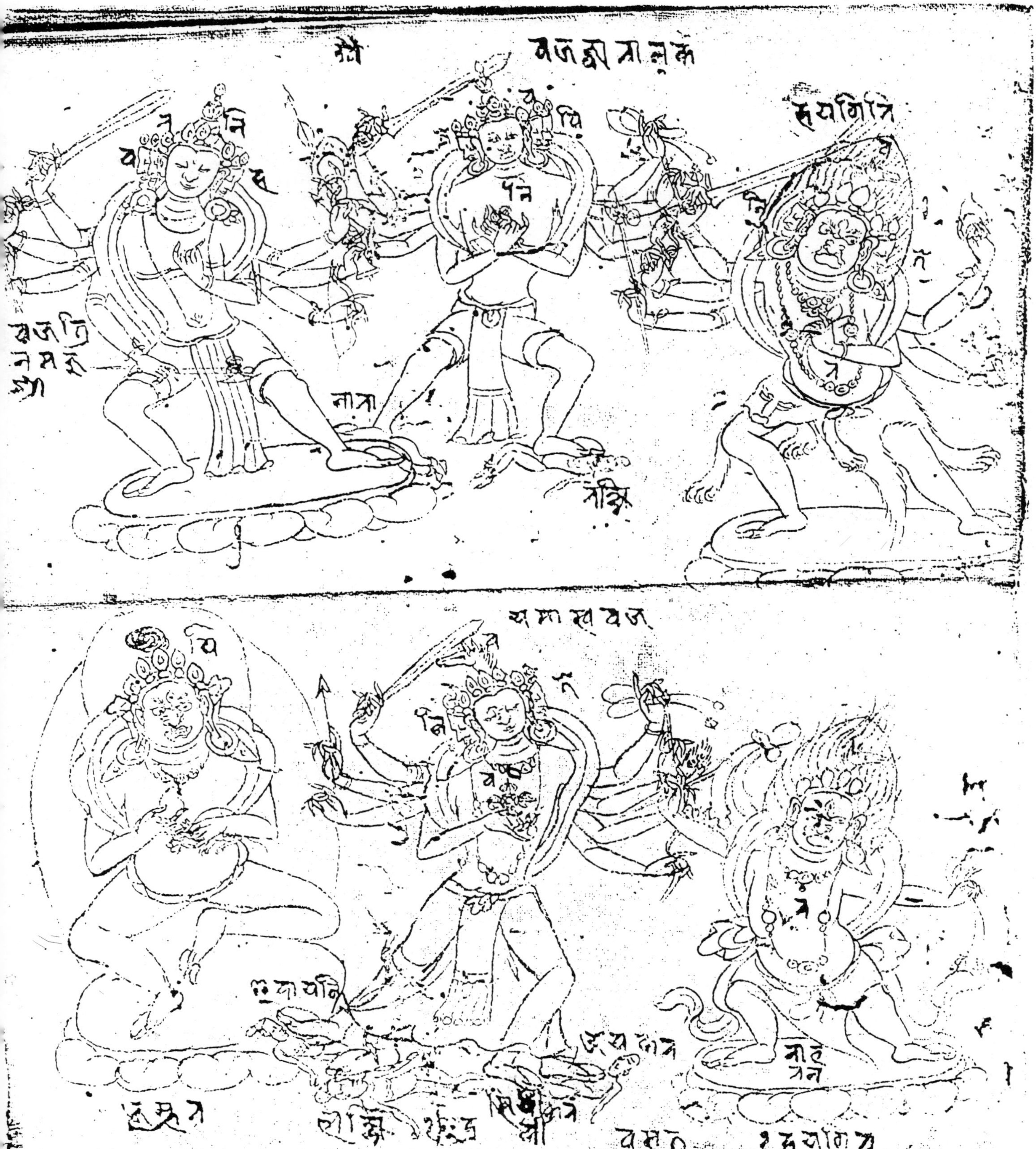

77 78 79

80 81 82

83 84 85

86 87 88 89

90 91 92 93

94 95

96 97 98 99

100 101 102 103

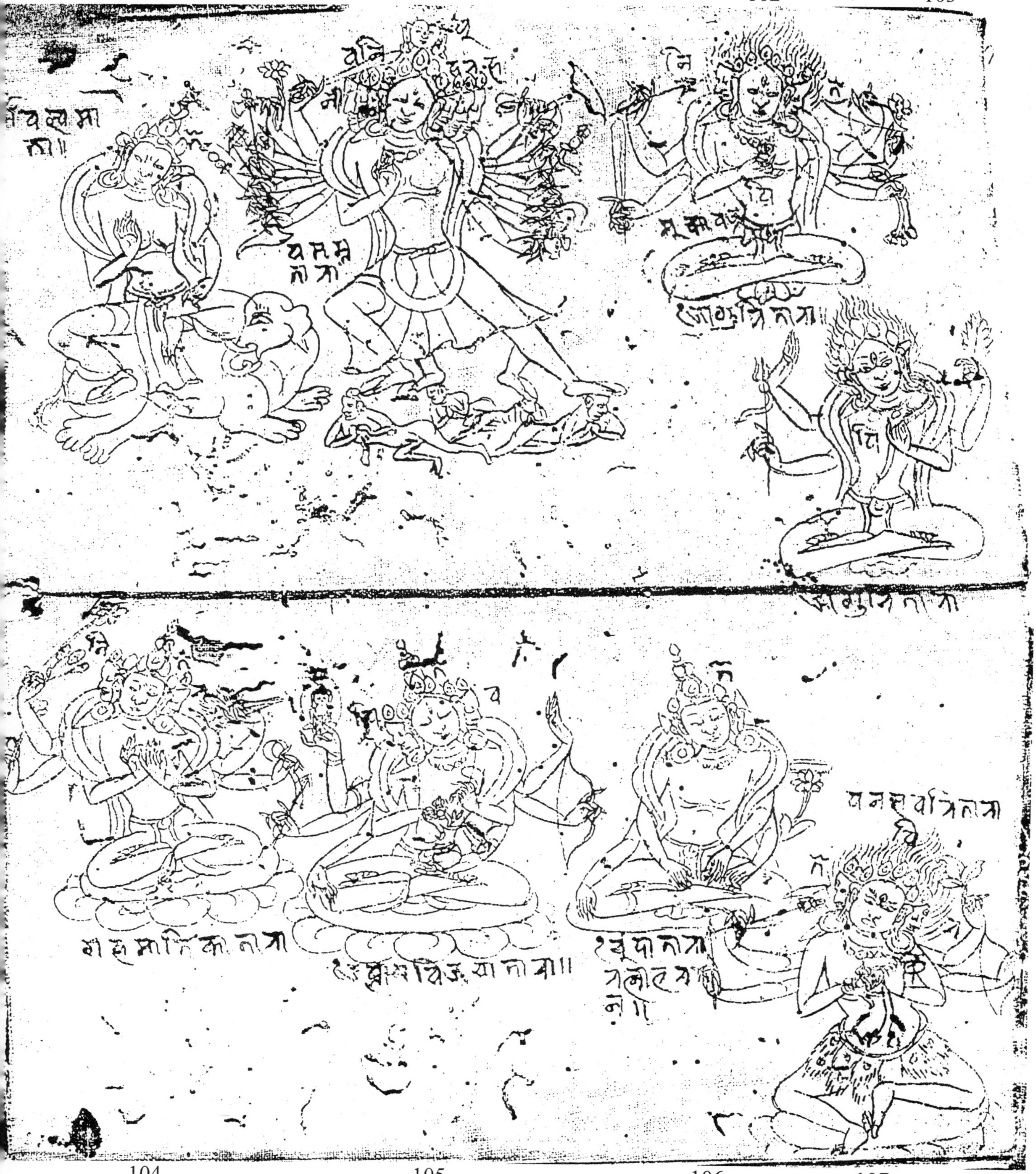

104 105 106 107

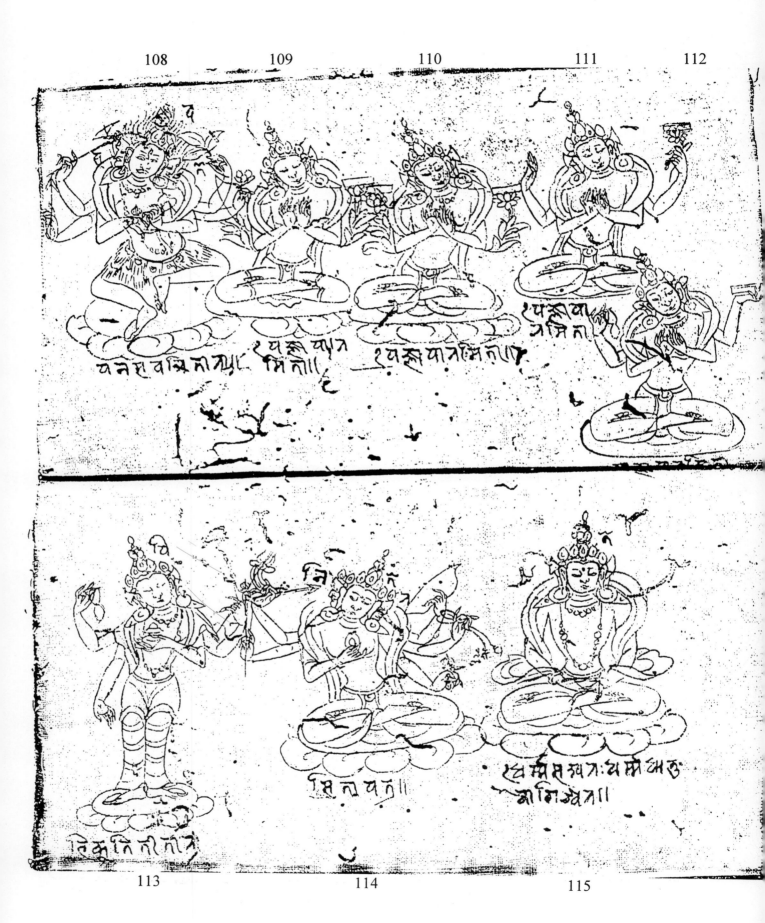

108 109 110 111 112

113 114 115

116 117 118 119

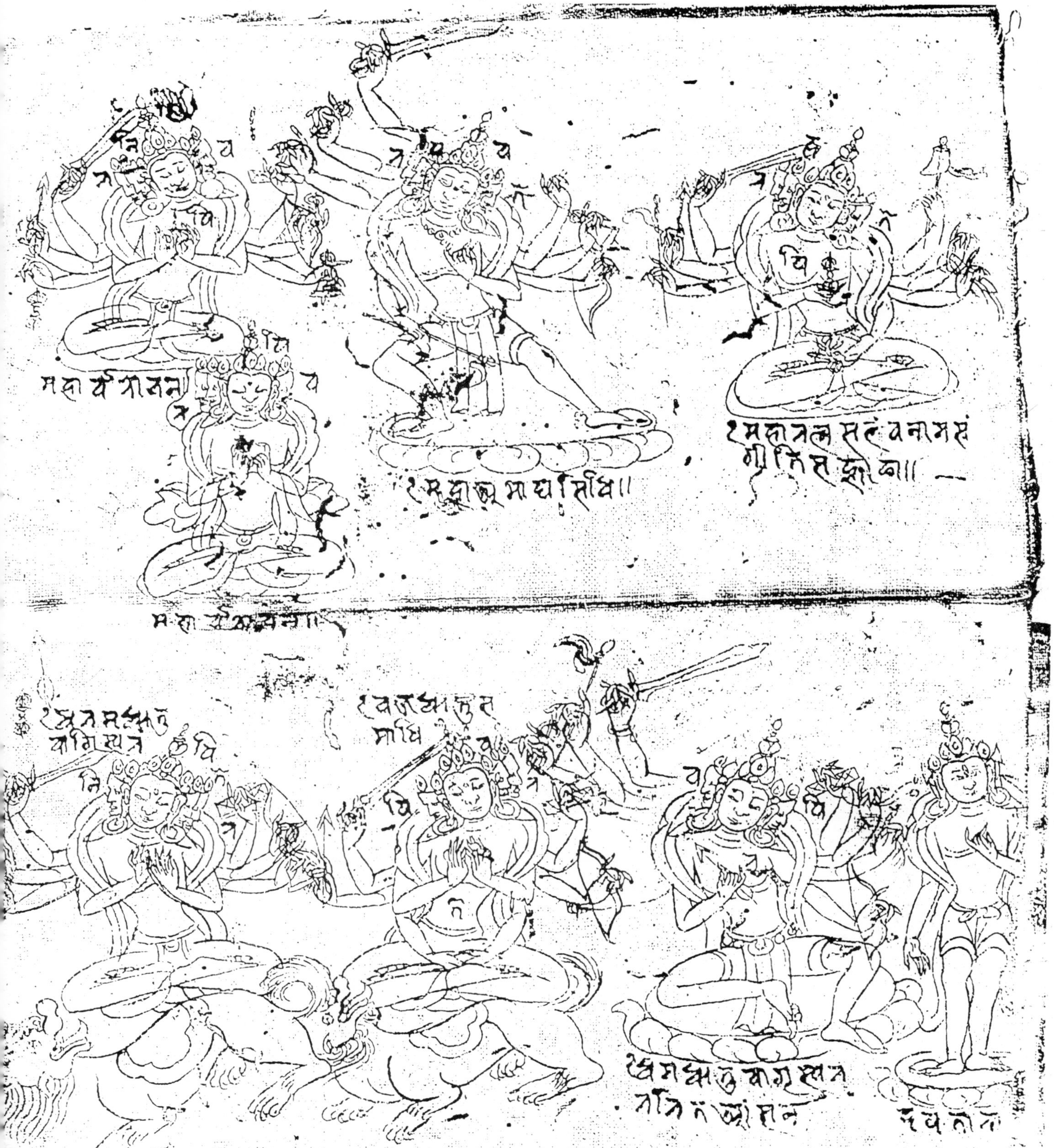

120 121 122 123

124 125 126

127 128 129 130

131 132 133

134 135 136

137 138 139

140 141 142

143 144 145

146 147 148

149 150 151

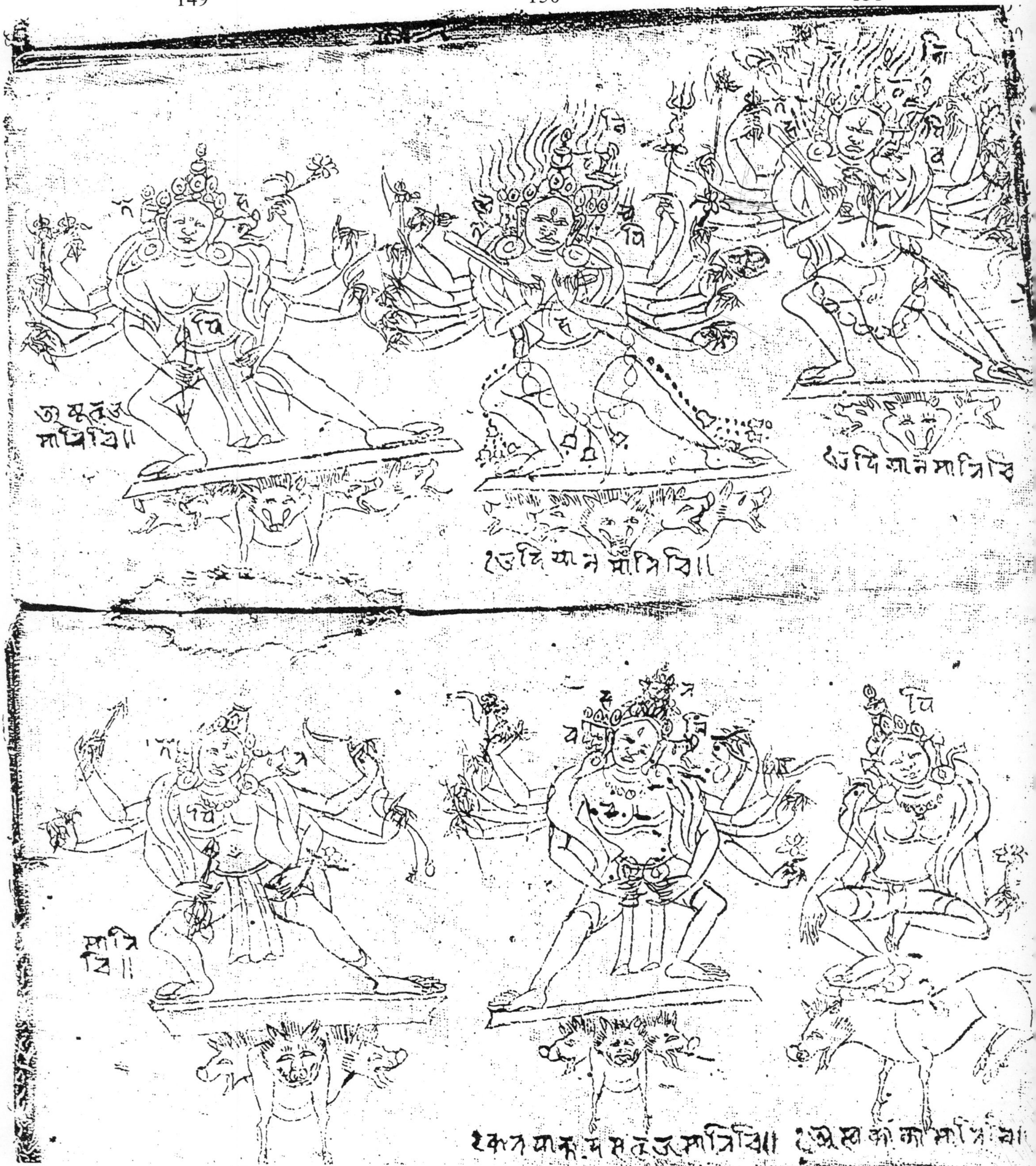

152 153 154

155

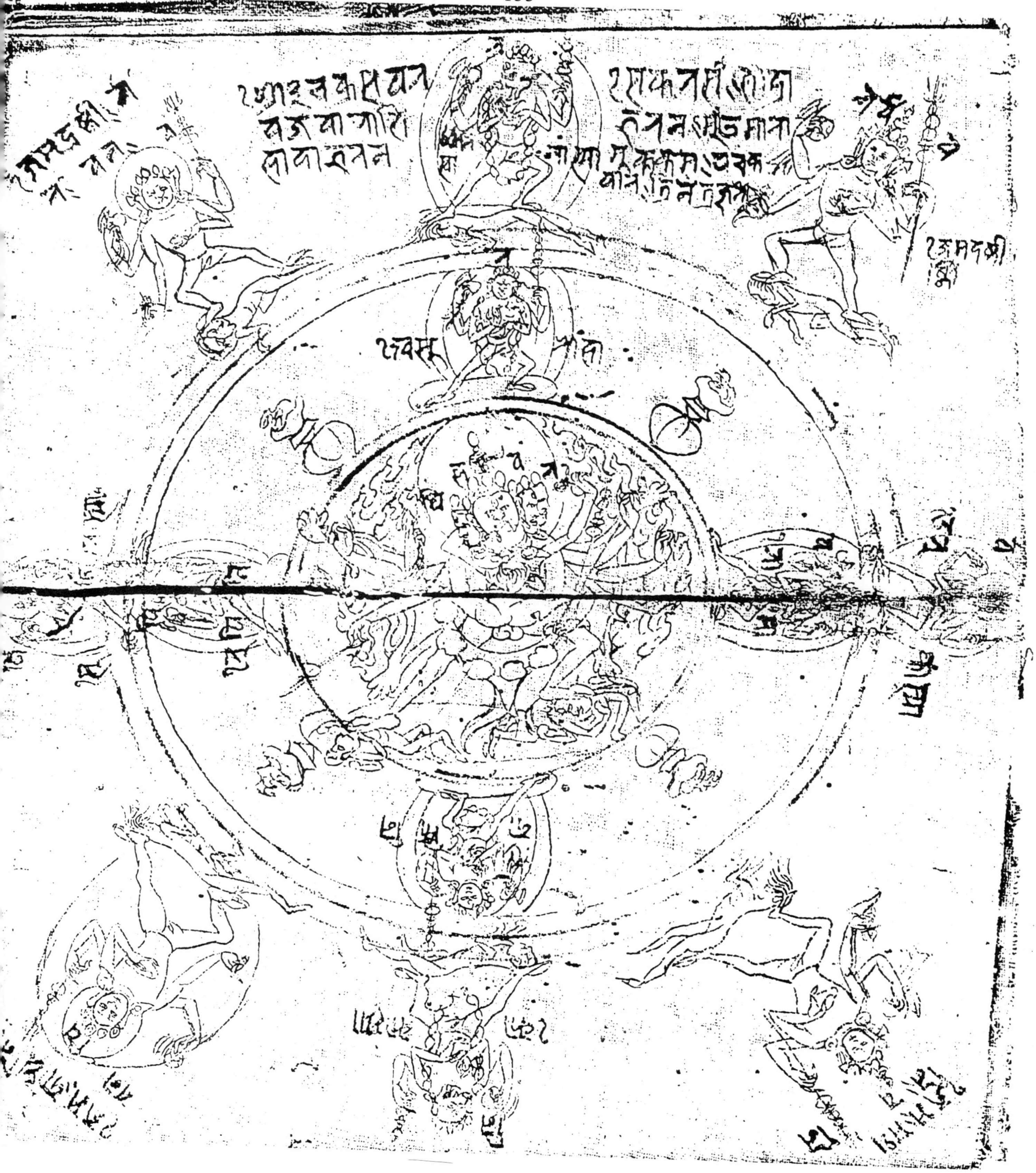

157 158 159

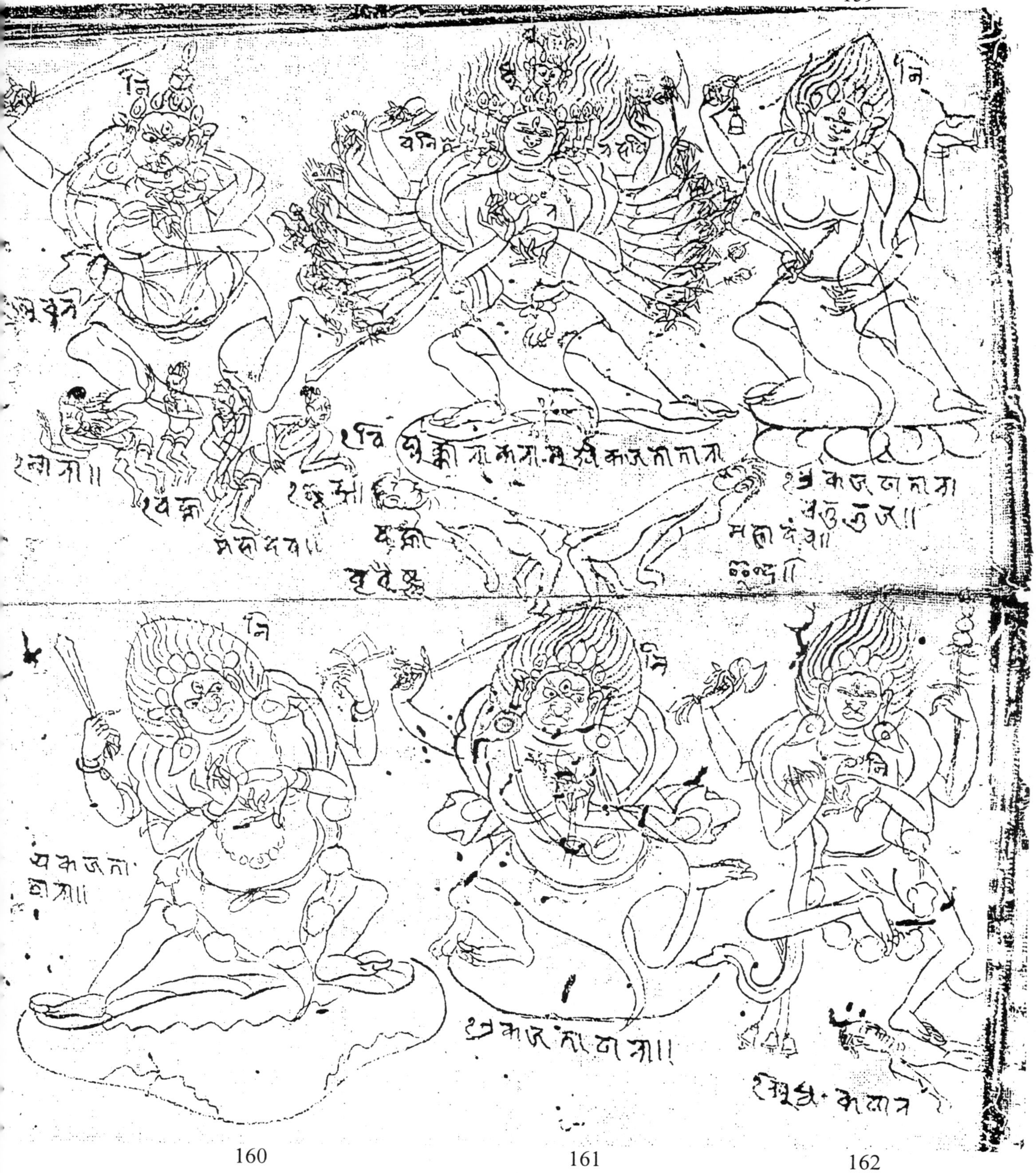

160 161 162

163 164 165

166 167 168

169 170 171

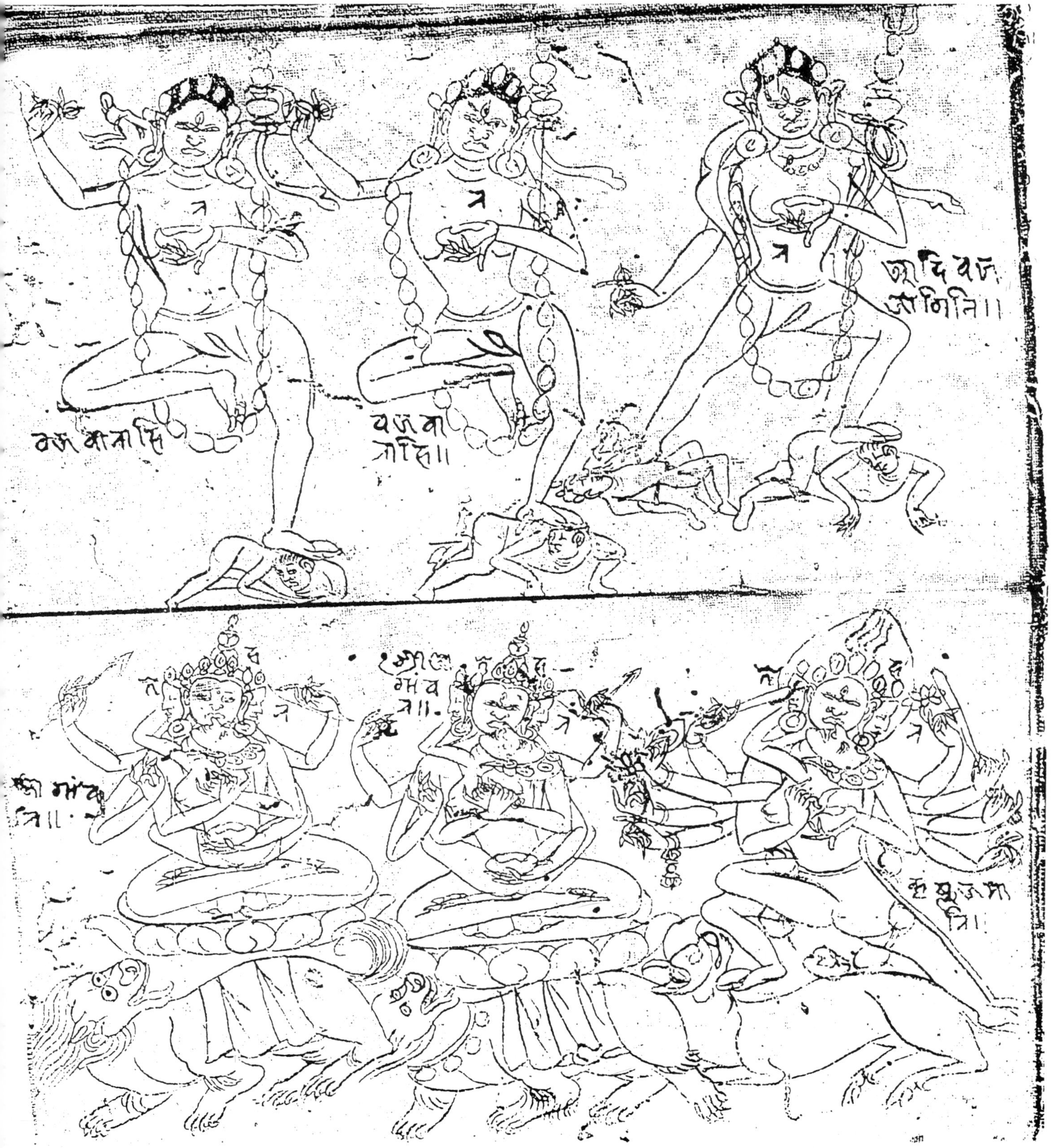

172 173 174

175 176 177

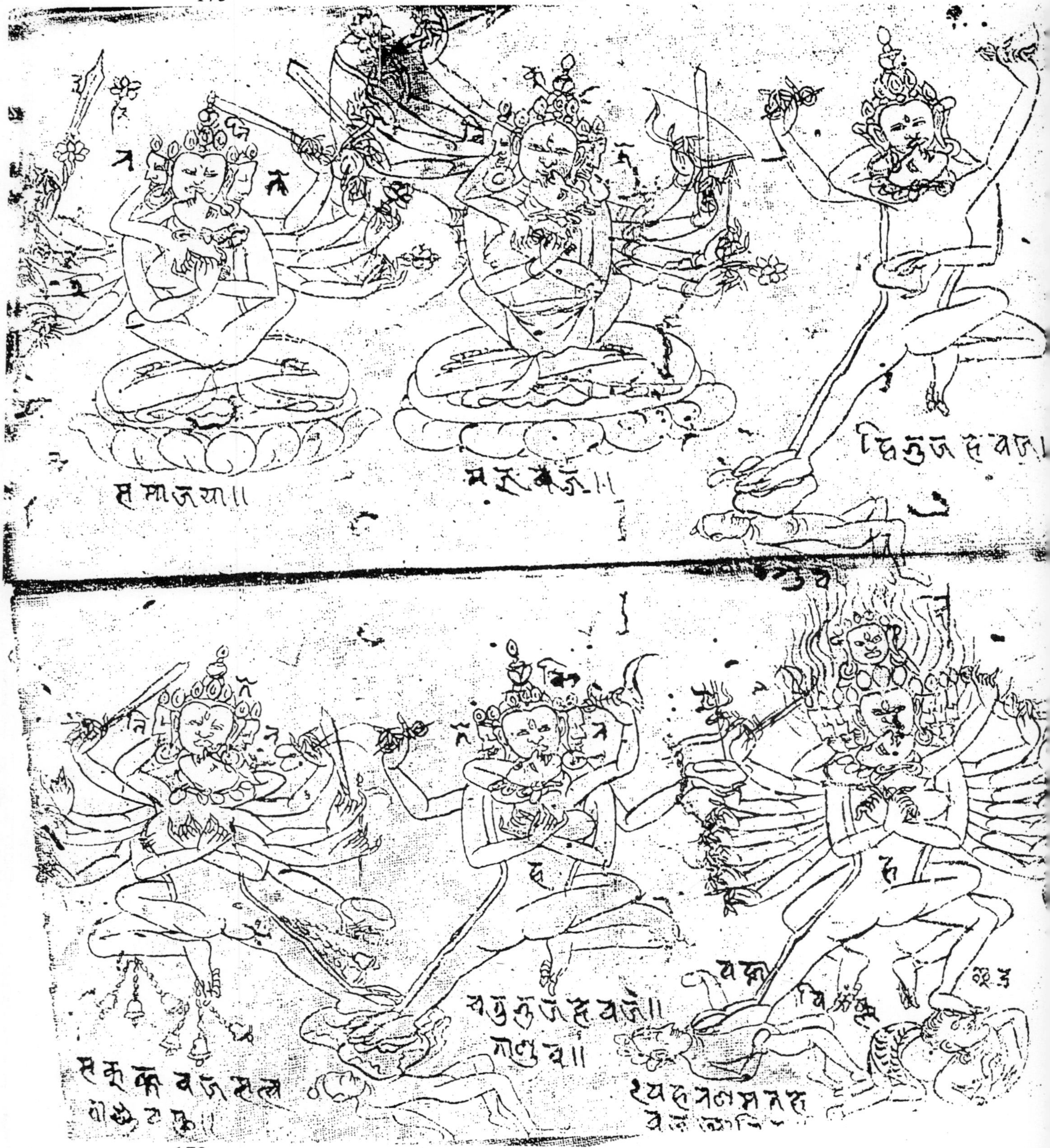

178 179 180

181 182 183

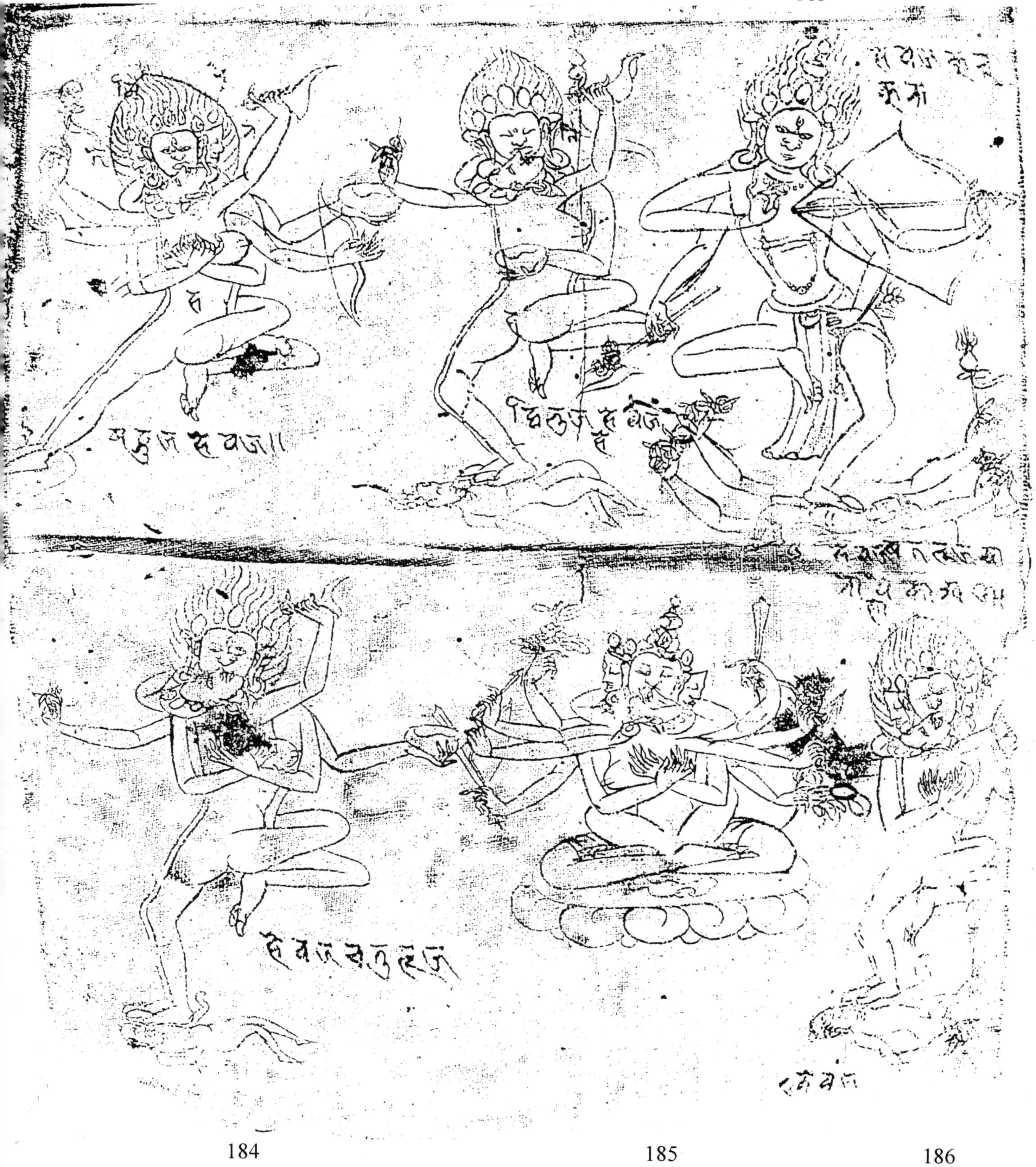

184 185 186

Table 2: The Iconographic Features of the Deities in the LC

No.	Name	Arms	Heads	Posture	Seat/Mount	Remarks
1	Unnamed	10	3	seated	lotus	in union with consort; BDC 125
2	Pratisarā	10	3	seated	lotus	BDC 124
3	Sāhasrapramardanī	6	3	seated	lotus	BDC 126
4	Māyūrī	2	1	seated	lotus	BDC 127
5	Mantrānusāraṇī	4	1	seated	lotus	BDC 128
6	Sitavatī	4	1	seated	lotus	BDC 129
7	Pratisarā	8	4	seated	lotus	BDC 130
8	Mahāmāyūrī	6	3	seated	lotus	BDC 131
9	Sāhasrapramardanī	6	3	seated	lotus	BDC 132
10	Śītavatī	4	3	seated	lotus	BDC 133: Sitavatī
11	Mantrānusāraṇī	4	1	seated	lotus	BDC 134
12	Mahāpratisarā	12	3	seated	lotus	BDC 135 (four-headed)
13	Mahāsāhasrapramardanī	10	4	seated	men	BDC 136
14	Mahāmāyūrī	8	3	seated	lotus	BDC 137
15	Mahāsaṃvara	many	11 (?)	standing	two deities	in union with consort
16	<Kamaṇḍalu-Lokeśvara '1'>	6	1	standing	–	BDC 49
17	<Jñānadhātu> '2'	6	1	standing	–	BDC 50
18	Āryāvalokiteśvara '3'	2	1	standing	–	BDC 48
19	<Nṛtyanātha '4'>	10	1	dancing	–	BDC 51
20	Vṛdāyaka '5'	4	1	standing	–	BDC 13
21	Śaṅkharanātha '6'	6	1	seated	Mahādeva riding a bull	BDC 14: Śaṅkhanātha

No.	Name	Arms	Heads	Posture	Seat/Mount	Remarks
22	Vajrahūtaka ‘7’	16	1	dancing	lotus?	BDC 16
23	<Viṣṇukānta ‘8’>	4	1	seated	Viṣṇu riding Garuḍa who is on a lotus	BDC 15
24	Kṛtāñjali ‘9’	12	1	standing	–	BDC 17
25	Uṣṇīṣa ‘10’	10	1	standing	lotus	BDC 19
26	Yamadaṇḍa ‘11’	4	1	standing	lotus	BDC 18
27	Sāntāsi ‘12’	6	1	standing	lotus	BDC 20: Śāntaśrī
28	Jñānadhātu ‘13’	6	1	seated	lotus	BDC 21
29	Śākyabuddha ‘14’	6	1	seated	lotus	BDC 22
30	Vajradhātu ‘15’	4	1	seated	lotus	BDC 23
31	Mañjunātha ‘16’	6	1	seated	lotus	BDC 24
32	Viśvahara ‘17’	6	1	seated	lotus	BDC 25
33	Dharmadhātu ‘18’	8	3	seated	horse on a lotus	BDC 26
34	Amitābha ‘19’	6	1	seated	elephant on a lotus	BDC 27
35	Mahāvajrasattva ‘20’	8	3	seated	lotus	BDC 28
36	Siṃhanātha ‘21’	6	1	seated	lotus	BDC 29
37	Halāhala[1] ‘22’	6	1	seated	lotus	with consort on left thigh; BDC 42
38	Sahasrabhuja ‘23’	8	11	standing	lotus	BDC 31
39	Dharmacakra ‘24’	10	3	seated	lotus	BDC 33
40	Ṣaḍakṣarī ‘25’	4	1	seated	lotus	BDC 34

[1] Halāhala is a Nevārī variant of Hālāhala.

No.	Name	Arms	Heads	Posture	Seat/Mount	Remarks
41	Acāta '26'	6	1	seated	lotus	BDC 35
42	Brahmadaṇḍa '27'	4	1	seated	lotus	with consort on left thigh
43	Kamalabhadra[2] '28'	8	3	seated	lotus	–
44	Kr̥ṣṇācala '29'	6	1	seated	lotus	–
45	Ratna/Rava___ (?)[3] '30'	6	1	seated	lotus	–
46	Pupala '31'	4	1	seated	lotus	BDC 36: Pupala-Mañjuśrī
47	Piṇḍapātra[4] '32'	4	1	seated	lotus	BDC 37
48	Prajñāpāramitā	6	1	seated	lotus	BDC 38: Tridaṇḍa
49	Prajñāpāramitā	4	1	seated	lotus	drawing inserted later; BDC 40
50	Prajñāpāramitā	4	1	seated	lotus	same form as 49
51	Prajñāpāramitā	2	1	seated	lotus	BDC 39
52	Prajñāpāramitā	2	1	seated	lotus	BDC 41
53	Prajñāpāramitā	4	1	seated	lotus	BDC 44
54	Prajñāpāramitā	4	1	seated	lotus	BDC 45
55	Arapacana-Mañjuśrī	2	1	seated	lotus	BDC 43, 2
56	Mañjuśrī	2	1	seated	lotus	BDC 46, 1
57	Siddhaikavīra-Mañjuśrī	2	1	seated	lotus	BDC 47
58	Vajrānaṅga-Mañjuśrī	6	1	standing	lotus	BDC 4
59	Vajrānaṅga-Mañjuśrī	4	1	standing	lotus	BDC 5
60	Vajrarāga-Mañjuśrī	2	1	seated	lotus	–

[2] The list of names in Lokesh Chandra 1984 reads the name as Kamalarudra.

[3] The reading is uncertain; the inscription can also be read as Lavaduvi (= Ravadevī?).

[4] The inscription reads Piṇḍapāta.

No.	Name	Arms	Heads	Posture	Seat/Mount	Remarks
61	Siddhaikavīra-Mañjuśrī	2	1	seated	lotus	BDC 7
62	Mahārājalīla-Mañjuśrī	2	1	seated	lion	BDC 8
63	Mañjuśrī	6	3	seated	lotus	–
64	Nāmasaṃgītisa lhāṅā[5] Mañjuśrī	4	3	seated	lotus	–
65	Ṣaḍakṣarī-Lokeśvara	4	1	seated	lotus	–
66	Halāhala-Lokeśvara	6	3	seated	lotus	with consort on left thigh
67	Vajradharma-Lokeśvara	2	1	seated	lotus, peacock	–
68	Ṣaḍakṣarī-Padmadhara	4	1	seated	lotus	BDC 6
69	Ṣaḍakṣarī	4	1	seated	lotus	–
70	Ṣaḍakṣarī-Maṇidhara	4	1	seated	lotus	–
71	Khasarpaṇa-Lokeśvara	2	1	seated	lotus	–
72	Siṃhanātha	2	1	seated	lotus	–
73	Harihari<hari>vāhana	6	1	seated	Hari riding Garuḍa who rides a lion	BDC 11
74	Trailokyavaśaṃkara-Lokeśvara	2	1	seated	lotus	–
75	<Lokanātha-Lokeśvara>	2	1	seated	lotus	BDC 52
76	Raktāryāvalo<kite>śvara	4	1	seated	lotus	–
77	Nīlakaṇṭha-Lokeśvara	2	1	seated	lotus, snakes	BDC 9
78	<Māyājālakrama-Krodha-Lokeśvara>	12	1	standing	lotus	BDC 53

[5] The inscription is hard to decipher. Nāmasaṃgītisa lhāṅā means 'mentioned in the Nāmasaṃgīti;' cf. no. 132, Mahāratnasaṃbhava *nāmasaṃgītisa lhāṅā*. Cf. Sādhanamālā 82 for Āryanāmasaṃgīti.

No.	Name	Arms	Heads	Posture	Seat/Mount	Remarks
79	Sugatisaṃdarśana-Lokeśvara	6	1	standing	lotus	BDC 54
80	Pretasaṃtarpita-Lokeśvara	6	1	standing	lotus	with two Pretas; BDC 56
81	Amoghapāśa-Lokeśvara	7 (!)[6]	1	standing	lotus	–
82	Harihari<hari>vāhanod-bhava-Lokeśvara	6	1	seated	Hari riding Garuḍa who rides a lion	BDC 12
83	Sahasrabhuja	many	11 (?)	standing	–	with one kneeling figure each right and left
84	Amoghapāśa-Lokeśvara	8	1	standing	–	BDC 55
85	Sukhāvatī-Lokeśvara	6	1	seated	lotus	BDC 59
86	Unnamed	8	11 (?)	standing	lotus	–
87	Padmanr̥tyeśvara	2	1	seated	lotus	with consort on left thigh; BDC 57
88	Padmanr̥tyeśvara	16	1	dancing	lotus	–
89	<Gaṇapa>	4	1	dancing	lotus?	BDC 58
90	Mahārāga-Mañjuśrī	8	4	seated	lotus	BDC 64
91	Mahākāla	4	1	seated	men on a lotus	BDC 63
92	Mahākāla	2	1	standing	back of man	BDC 60
93	Maitrī (= Maitreya)	4	3	seated	lotus	BDC 61
94	Maitrī (= Maitreya)	2	1	seated	lotus	BDC 62
95	Mañjuśrī	2	1	seated	lotus	BDC 65

[6] Four arms are shown on the right and three on the left side. One arm was apparently added later on the right side.

No.	Name	Arms	Heads	Posture	Seat/Mount	Remarks
96	Mahākāla	2	1	standing	lotus	BDC 66
97	Vajratīkṣṇa-Mañjuśrī	2	1	seated	lotus	BDC 67
98	Vajrakhaḍga-Mañjuśrī	2	1	seated	lotus	BDC 68
99	Prajñājñāna-Mañjuśrī	2	1	seated	lotus	BDC 69
100	Jñānakāya-Mañjuśrī	2	1	seated	lotus	BDC 70
101	Vāgīśvara-Mañjuśrī	2	1	seated	lotus	BDC 71
102	Ādibuddha-Mañjuśrī	8	5	seated	lotus	BDC 72
103	Arapacana-Mañjuśrī	2	1	seated	lotus	–
104	Vajratīkṣṇa-Mañjuśrī[7]	8	4	standing	lotus	BDC 74
105	Mañjuśrī	2	1	seated	lotus	–
106	Caturtha-Vajrāmṛta[8] Amṛtakuṇḍalī	6	3	standing	Gaṇapati	BDC 73
107	Yamāśvavajra[9]	8	4	standing	Indra, Indrāyaṇī, Lakṣmī, Jayakara, Siddhikara, Madhukara[10] and Vasanta	top head is a horse's head; four legs; BDC 78
108	Vajrajvālana<lār>ka	8	4	standing	Nārāyaṇa and Lakṣmī	BDC 75

[7] The inscription reads 'Vajratrīkṣṇa-Mañjuśrī.'

[8] I.e., the fourth (*caturtha*) Vajrāmṛta named Amṛtakuṇḍalī in a group of four; cf. the reference in Niṣpannayogāvalī p. 19, 11 with three other Vajrāmṛta deities in the Vajrāmṛtatantra.

[9] The deity has similar characteristics to Paramāśva; cf. the descriptions in Niṣpannayogāvalī, p. 60, 7–12 and Sādhanamālā 261.

[10] The three names Jayakara, Siddhikara and Madhukara are written as Jayakra, Siddhikra and Madhukra.

No.	Name	Arms	Heads	Posture	Seat/Mount	Remarks
109	Hayagrīva	2	2	standing	lotus	top head is a horse's head; BDC 79
110	Hayagrīva	6	4	standing	lotus	top head is a horse's head; BDC 76
111	Hayagrīva	8	4	dancing ?	lotus	top head is a horse's head; BDC 80
112	Jambhala	2	1	seated	lotus	BDC 77
113	Ucchuṣma-Jambhala	2	1	standing	back of man	BDC 81
114	Mahājambhala	6	3	seated	lotus	in union with consort; BDC 82
115	Vasudhārā	2	1	seated	lotus	BDC 83
116	Vasudhārā	2	1	seated	lotus	BDC 84
117	Vasudhārā	6	1	seated	lotus	BDC 85
118	Dhvajāgrakeyūra	4	3 (?)	standing	lotus	BDC 91 (four-headed)
119	Vajraśr̥ṅkhalā	6	3	seated	lotus	–
120	Vajraśr̥ṅkhalā	8	3	standing	lotus	–
121	Vajravīṇā-Sarasvatī	2	1	standing	lotus	–
122	Mahāsarasvatī	2	1	standing	lotus	–
123	Vajracarcikā[11]	6	1	standing	corpse	–
124	Aparājitā	2	1	standing	Gaṇeśa	–

[11] The list of deities' names in Lokesh Chandra 1984 reads Vajracaṇḍikā. The inscription reads Vajracaṃjikā. The goddess Vajracarcikā is described in Sādhanamālā 193. For a similar line drawing, see the Nepalese sketchbook M.84.171.3 a-g preserved in the Los Angeles County Museum of Art.

No.	Name	Arms	Heads	Posture	Seat/Mount	Remarks
125	Dharmaśaṅkha-Dharmadhātu-Vāgīśvara	2	1	seated	lotus	BDC 115
126	Dharmadhātu-Vāgīśvara	8	3	seated	lotus	BDC 122
127	Da<ṃ>va-Tārā[12]	2	1	standing	lotus	BDC 123
128	Dharmadhātu-Vāgīśvara	8	4	seated	lotus on lion	BDC 120
129	Vajradhātu(samādhi)	8	4	seated	lotus on lion	BDC 121
130	Mahāvairocana	8	4	seated	lotus	BDC 116
131	Mahā-Amoghasiddhi	8	4	standing	lotus	BDC 118
132	Mahāratnasaṃbhava *nāmasaṃgītisa lhāṅā*[13]	8	4	seated	lotus	BDC 119
133	Mahāvairocana	2	4	seated	lotus	BDC 117
134	Grahamātr̥kā	6	3	seated	lotus	BDC 104: Grahamātr̥kā Tārā
135	Uṣṇīṣavijayā	8	3	seated	lotus	BDC 105: Uṣṇīṣavijayā Tārā
136	Cundā Tārā	4	1	seated	lotus	BDC 106
137	Parṇaśavarī Tārā	6	3	seated	lotus	BDC 107
138	Parṇaśavarī Tārā	6	3	seated	lotus	BDC 108
139	Prajñāpāramitā	2	1	seated	lotus	BDC 109
140	Prajñāpāramitā	2	1	seated	lotus	BDC 110
141	Prajñāpāramitā	4	1	seated	lotus	BDC 111
142	Prajñāpāramitā	4	1	seated	lotus	BDC 112
143	Bhr̥kuṭī Tārā	4	1	standing	lotus	BDC 113
144	Sitātapatrā	6	3	seated	lotus	BDC 114

[12] The word *daṃva* means 'standing' in Nevārī.

[13] The inscription *nāmasaṃgītisa lhāṅā* means 'told in the Nāmasaṃgīti.'

No.	Name	Arms	Heads	Posture	Seat/Mount	Remarks
145	Mahācīnakrama-Tārā	4	1	standing	corpse	–
146	Sita-Tārā	2	1	seated	lotus	–
147	Sita-Tārā	4	1	seated	lotus	–
148	Sita-Ṣaḍbhuja-Tārā	6	3	seated	lotus	–
149	Jāṅgulī Tārā	4	1	seated	lotus	–
150	Dhanada-Tārā	4	1	seated	lotus	–
151	Durgottāraṇī Tārā	4	1	seated	lotus	–
152	Viśvamātā	2	1	seated	elephant on a lotus	BDC 100
153	Prasanna-Tārā	16	8	standing	Brahmā, Nārāyaṇa, Rudra and Indra	four legs; BDC 101
154	Jāṅgulī Tārā	6	3	seated	lotus	BDC 102
155	Jāṅgulī Tārā	4	1	seated	lotus	BDC 103
156	Dhvajāgrakeyūrī	4	4	standing	lotus	–
157	Sragdharā Tārā	2	1	standing	lotus	with one attendant each right and left; BDC 95
158	Mahattarīpa-Tārā	2	1	seated	lotus	BDC 92
159	Varada-Tārā	2	1	seated	lotus	BDC 93
160	Māyūrī	2	1	seated	lotus	–
161	Aśoka-Tārā[14]	2	1	seated	lotus	BDC 94
162	Ekajaṭā	2	1	seated	lotus	–

[14] The inscription reads Aśvaka-Tārā. The letters *o* and *va* are often interchanged in Nevārī manuscripts.

No.	Name	Arms	Heads	Posture	Seat/Mount	Remarks
163	Jāṅgulī	2	1	seated	lotus	–
164	Bhadrāsana-Vaśyādhikāra-Tārā[15]	2	1	seated	lotus	BDC 97
165	Vajra-Tārā	8	3	seated	lotus	BDC 98
166	Kiṃcidvistara-Tārā (i.e., Āryatārā)	2	1	seated	lotus	BDC 99
167	Mahāsarasvatī	6	3	standing	lotus	BDC 86
168	Vajraśāradā	2	1	standing	lotus	BDC 87
169	Vajrasarasvatī	2	1	seated	lotus	BDC 88
170	Vajradhāteśvarī[16]	2	1	seated	lotus	BDC 89
171	Pratyaṅgirā	6	1	seated	lotus	BDC 90

[15] Cf. Sādhanamālā 92 for this form of Tārā, who is seated in the *bhadrāsana*.

[16] The inscription reads 'Vajradhātateśvarī.' The correct Sanskrit word would be Vajradhātvīśvarī; the Nevārī variant Vajradhāteśvarī is also used in Williams/Tribe 2000: 211.

The Sketchbook LC

1

2 3

4 5 6

7 8 9

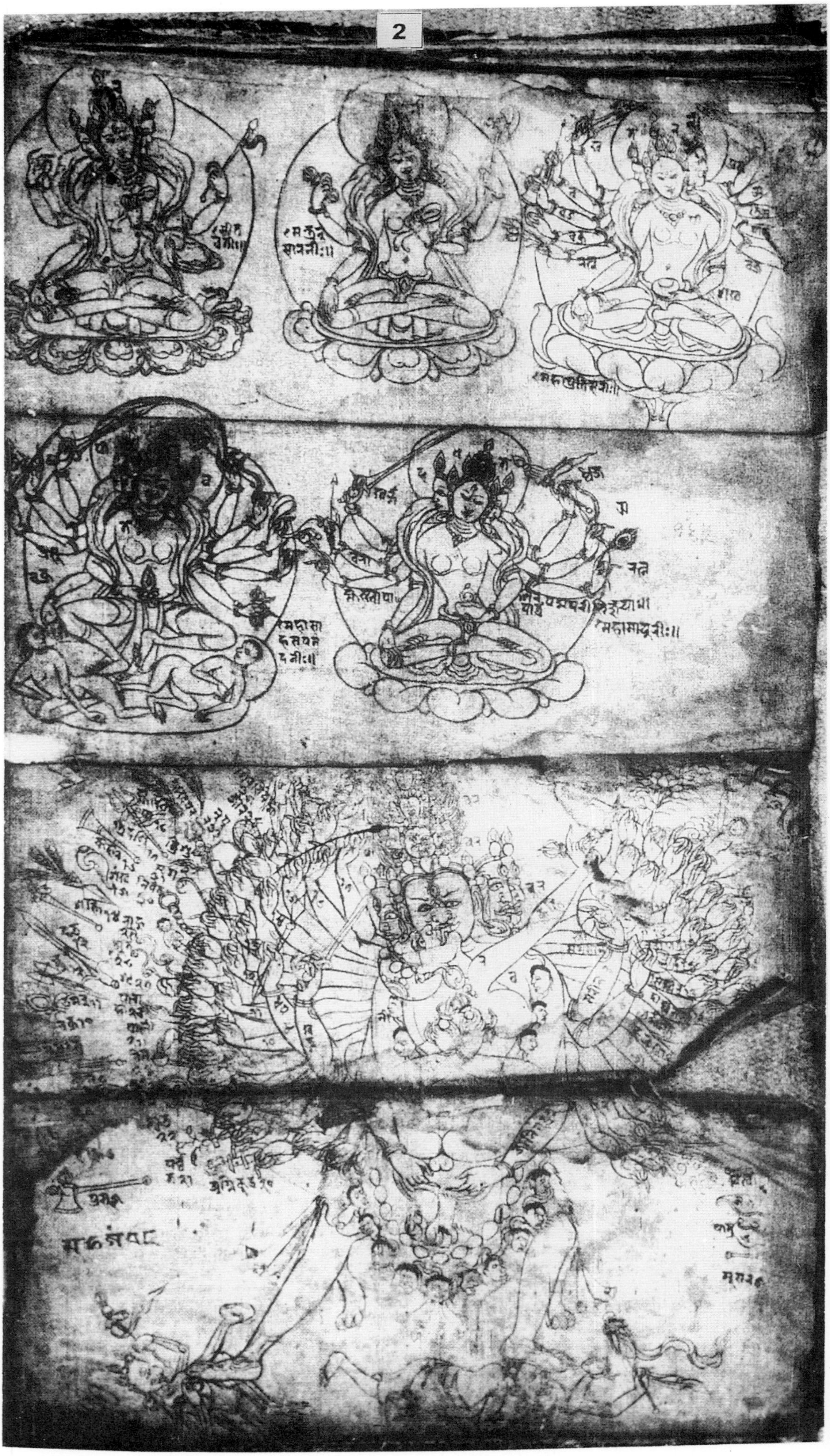

10 11 12

13 14

15

3

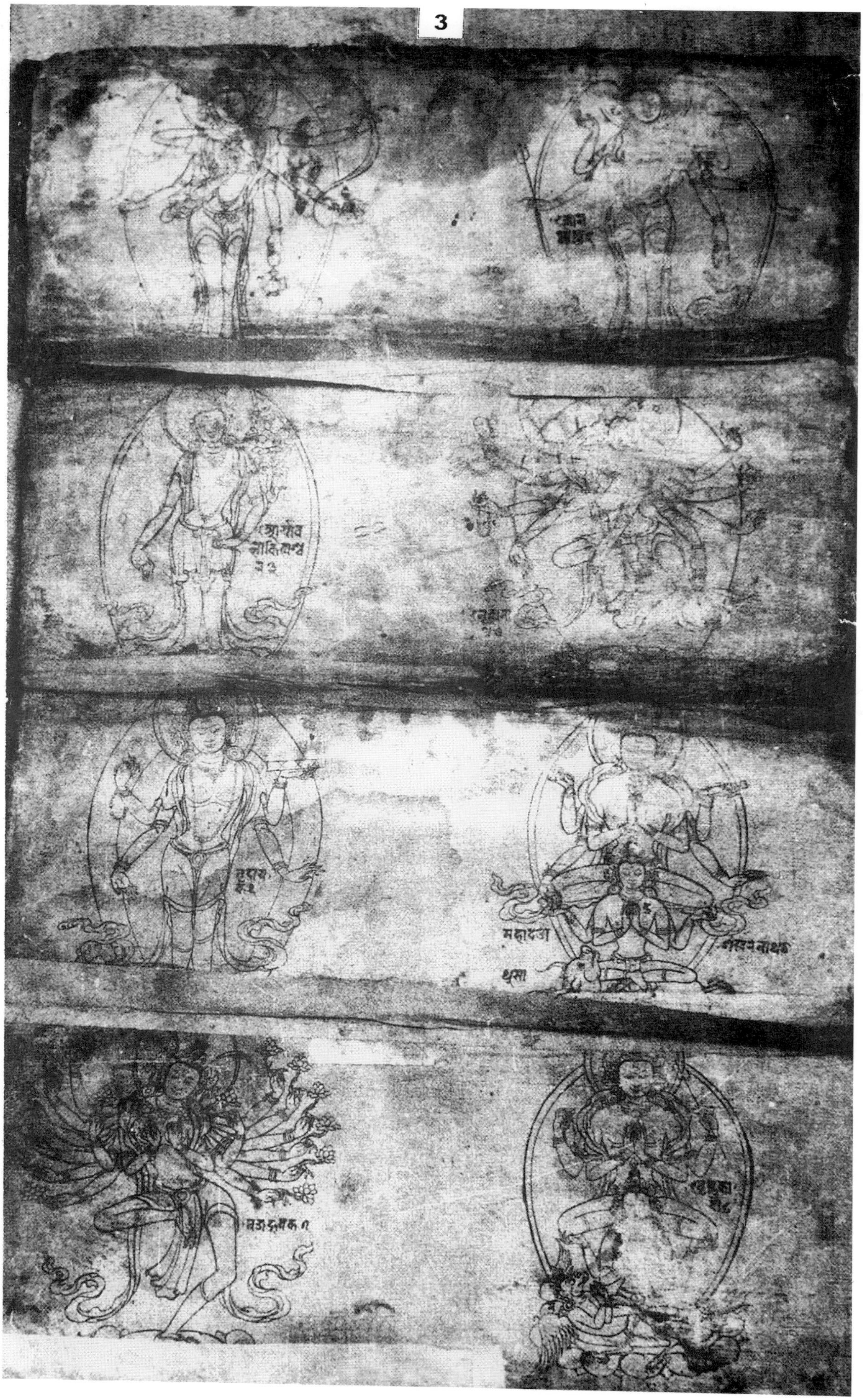

16 17

18 19

20 21

22 23

24 25

26 27

28 29

30 31

32 33

34 35

36 37

38 39

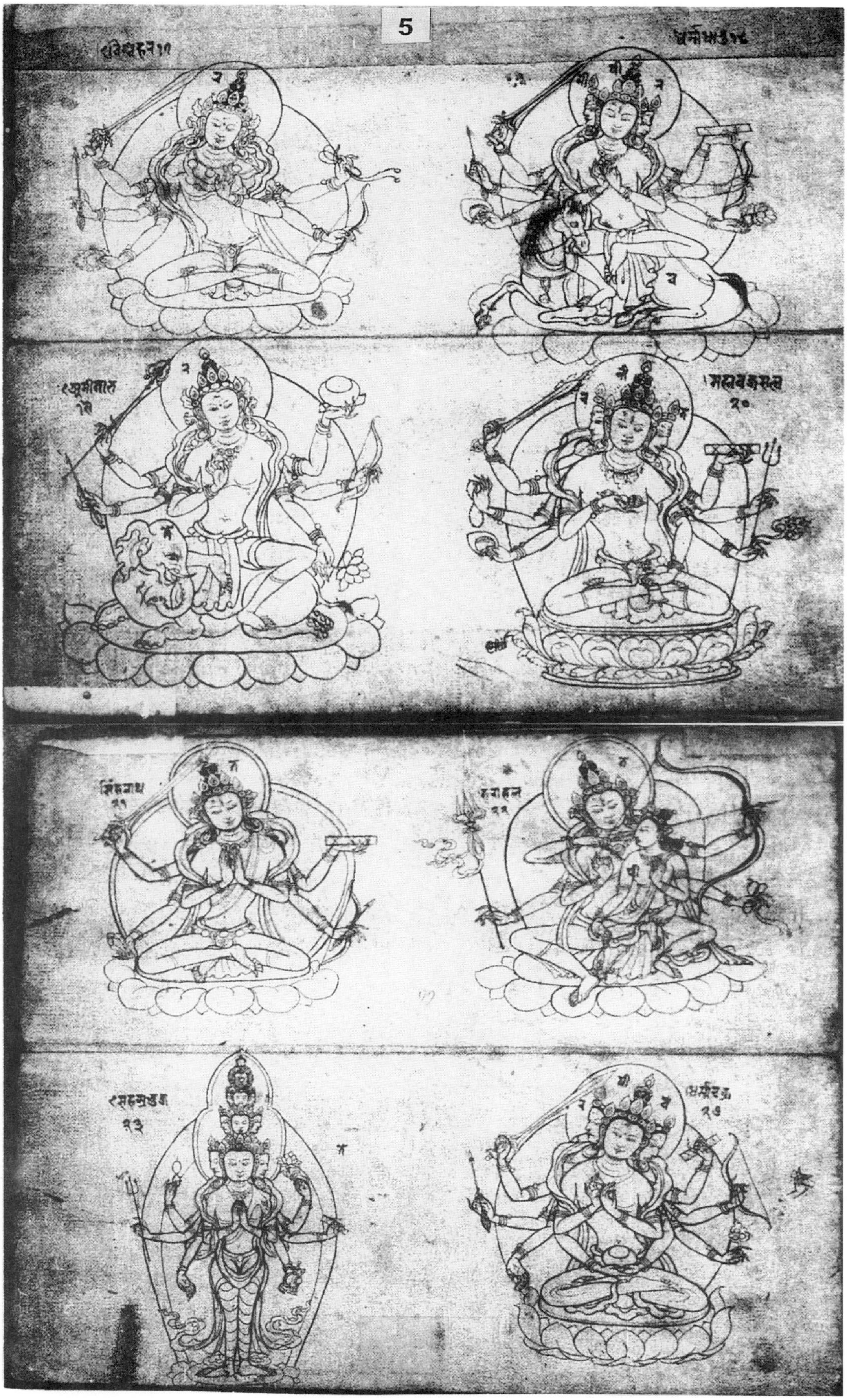

40 41

42 43

44 45

46 47

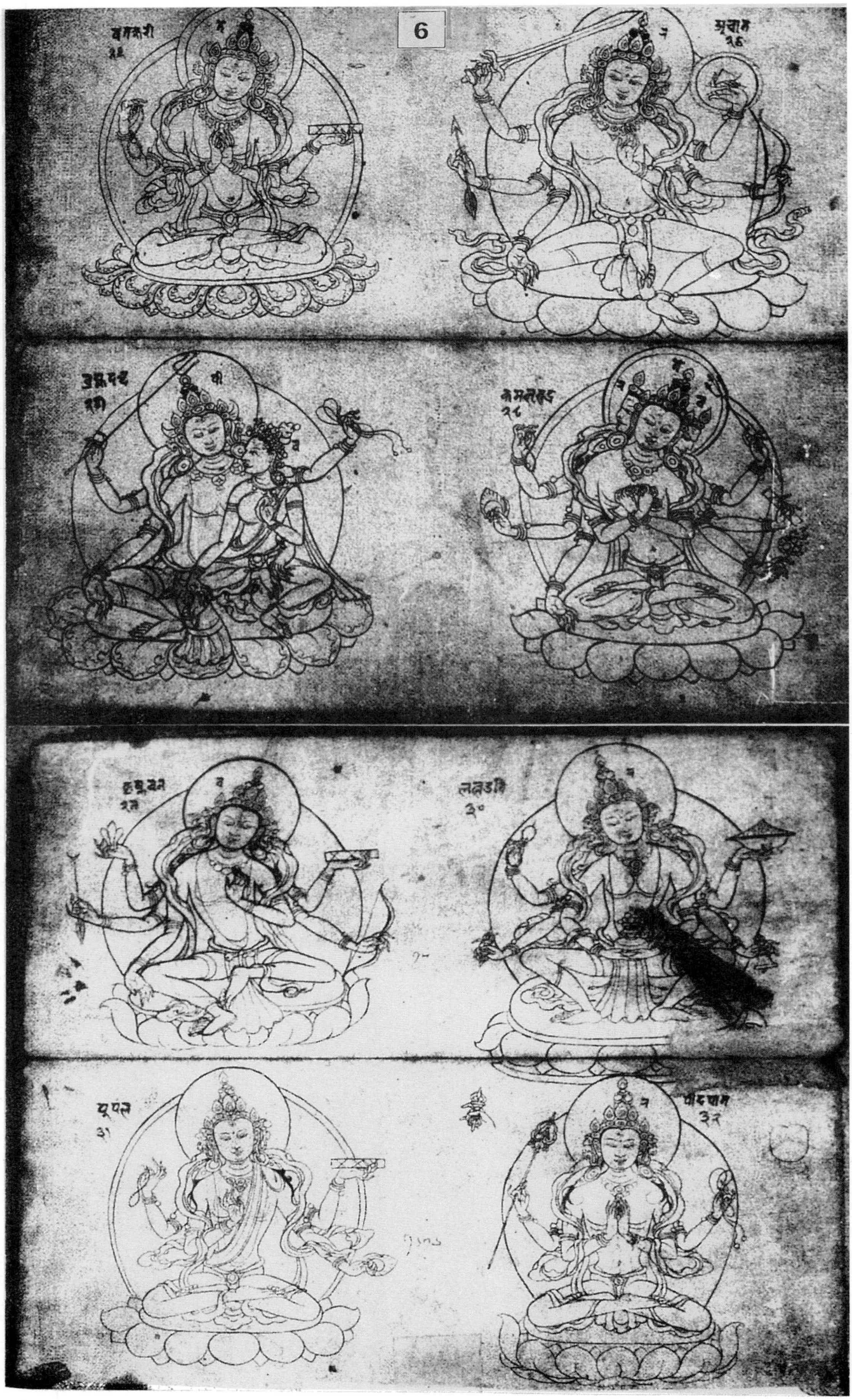

48 49

50 51 52

53 54 55

56 57

58 59

60 61 62

63 64 65

66 67 68

69 70 71

72 73 74

75 76 77

78 79

80 81

82 83 84

85 86 87

88 89

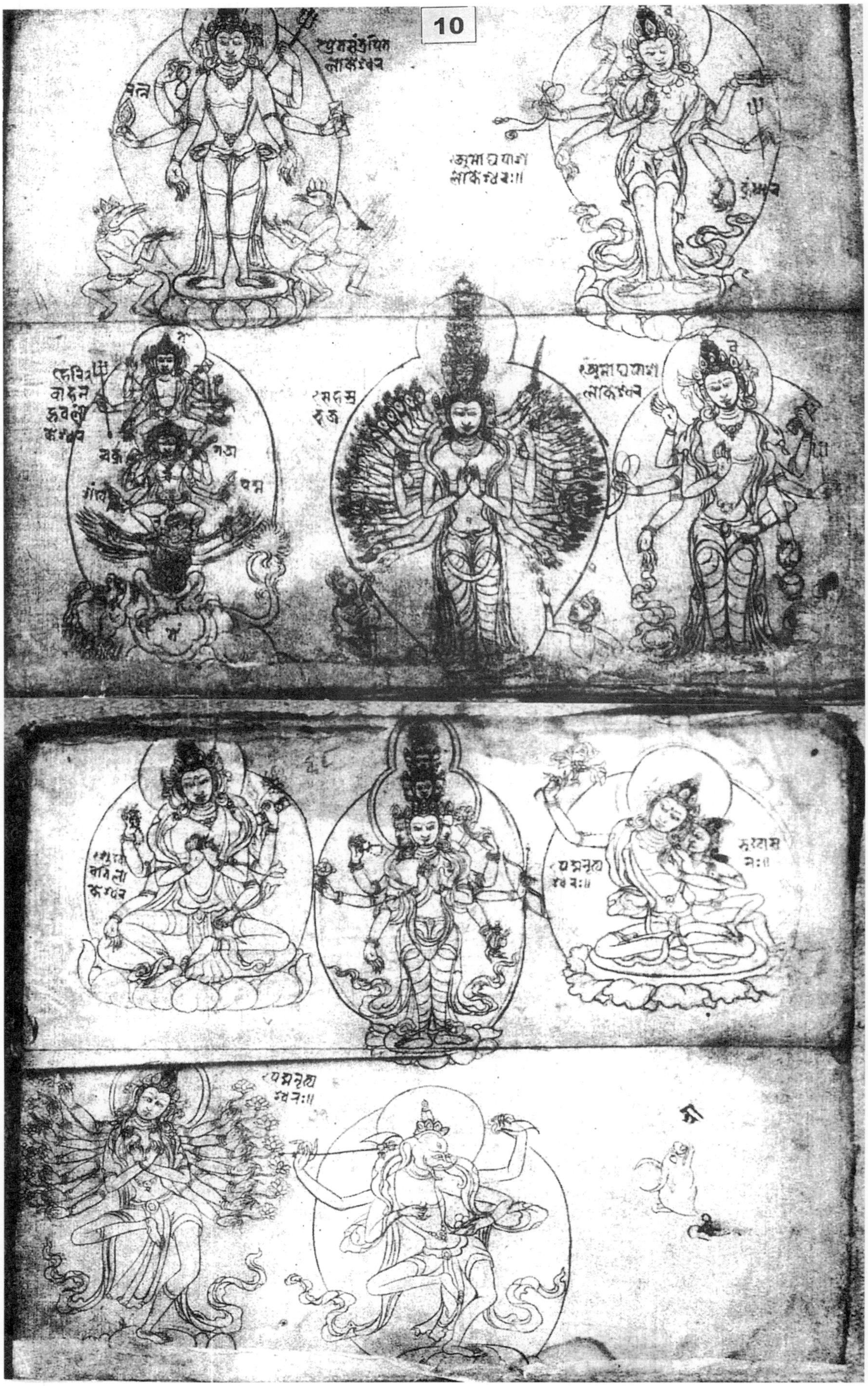

90 91

92 93 94

95 96 97

98 99 100

101 102 103

104 105 106

107 108

109 110

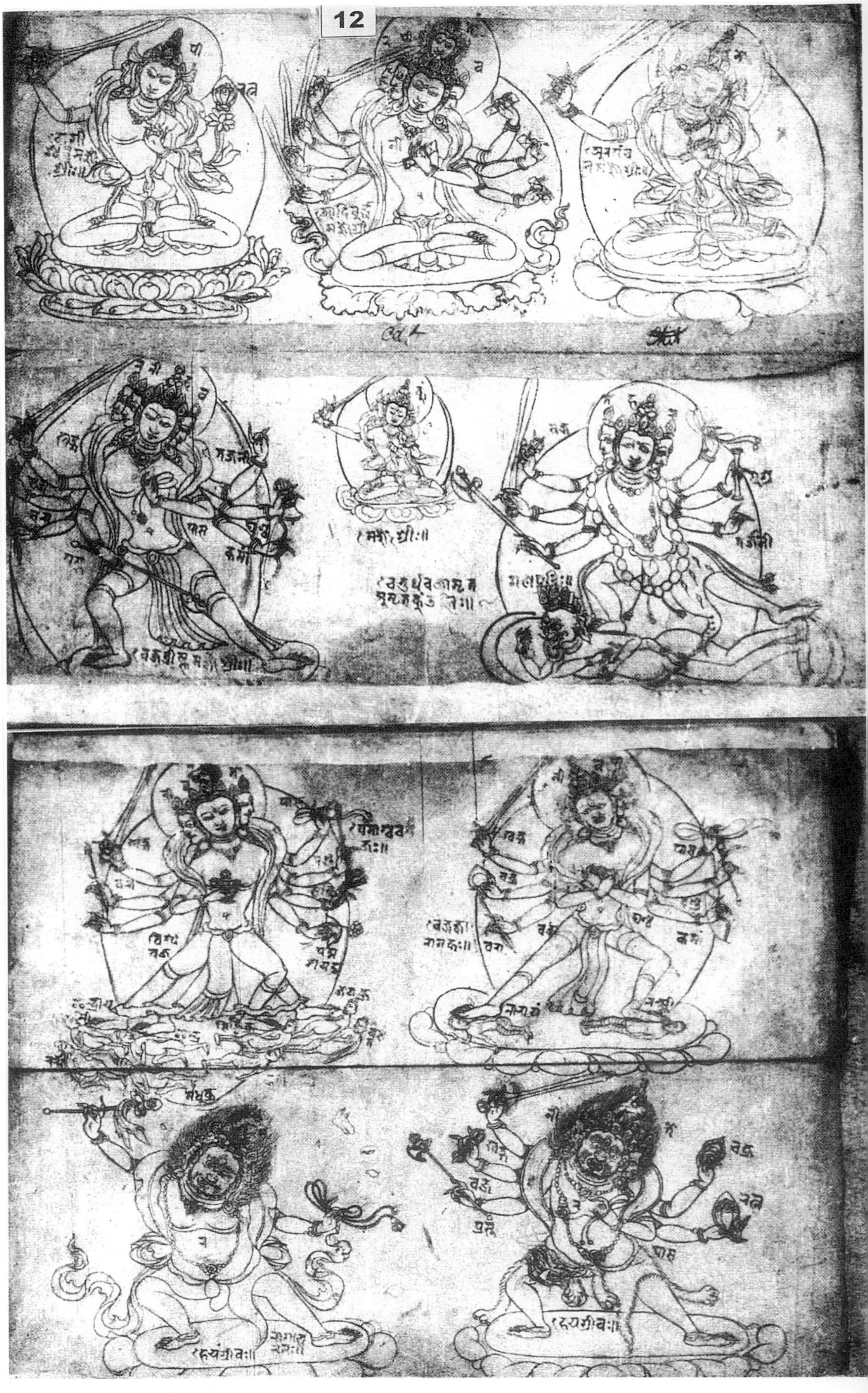

111 112

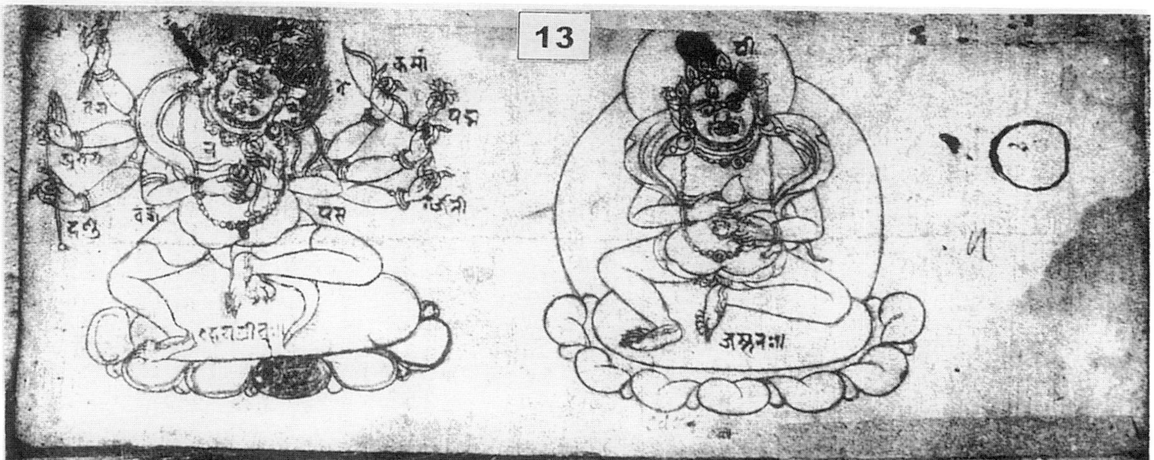

113 114

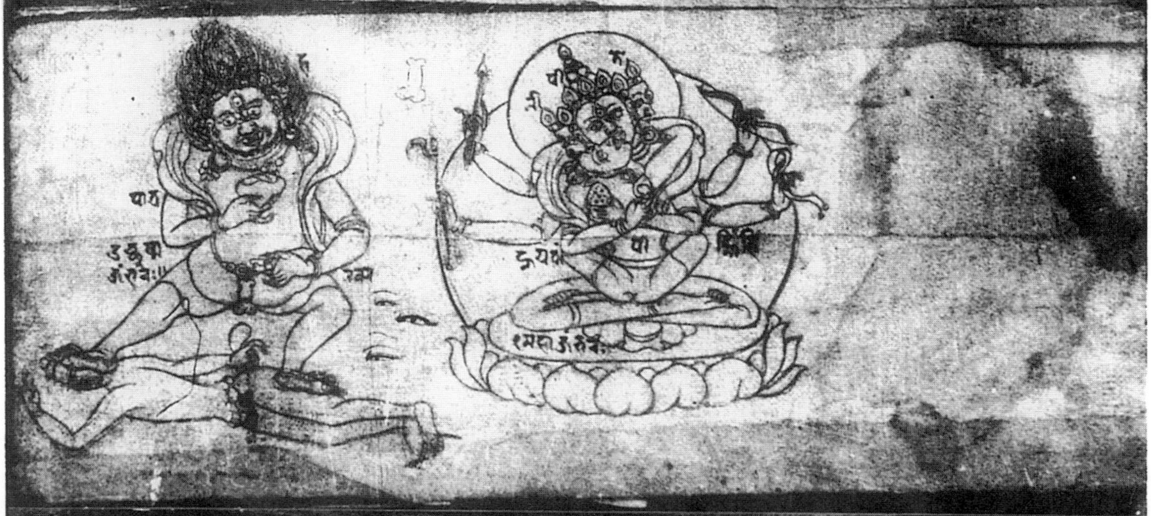

115 116 117

118 119

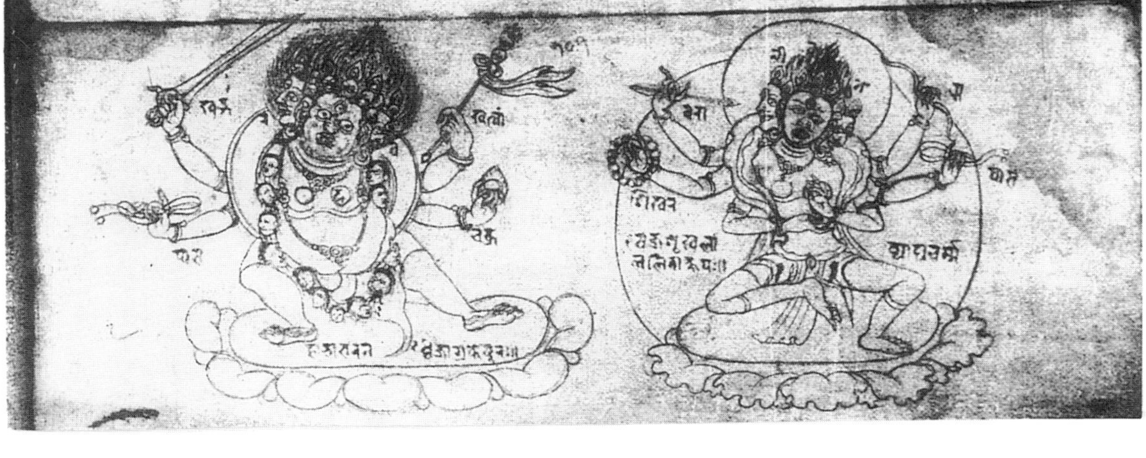

120 121 122

123 124

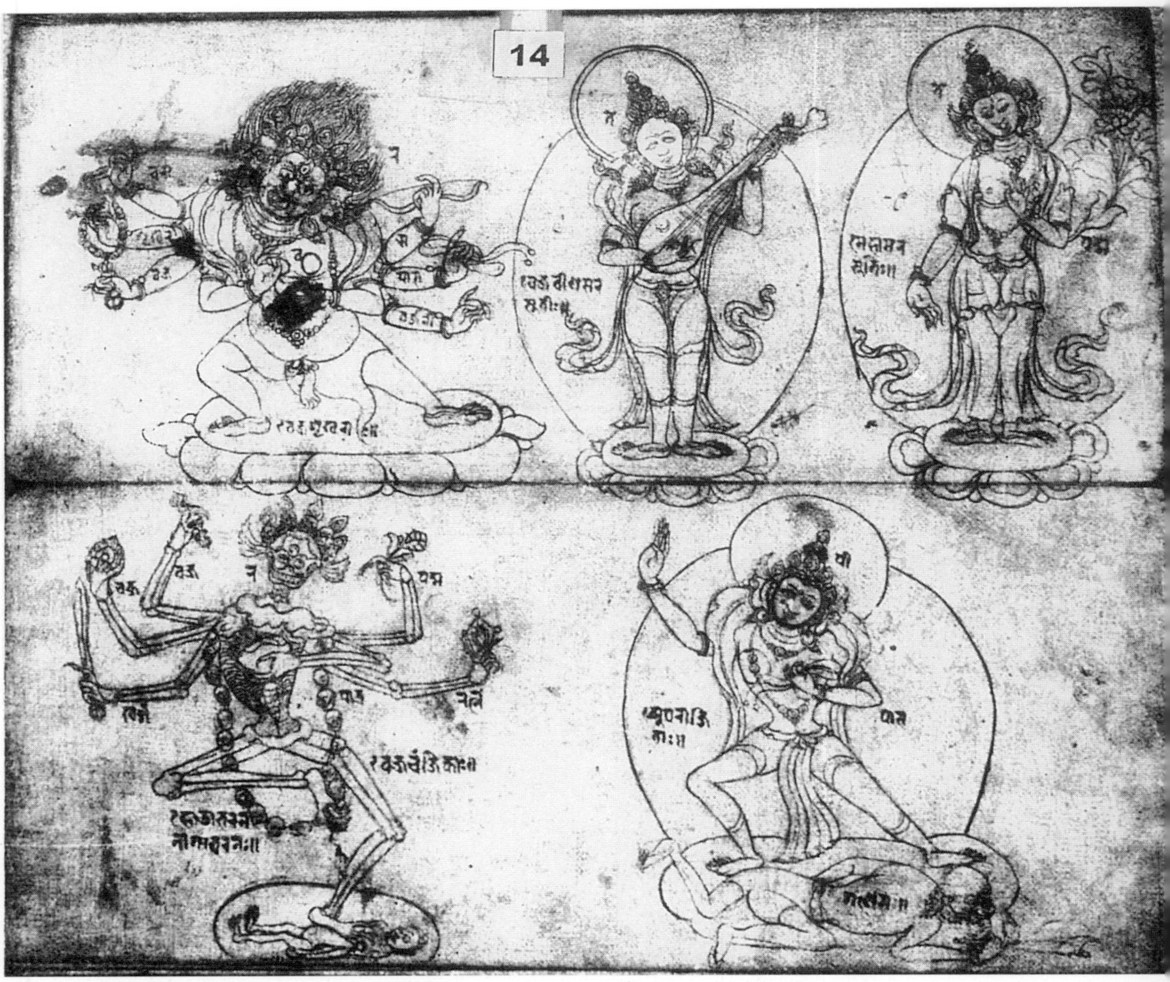

125 126 127

128 129

130 131

132 133

134 135 136

137 138 139

140 141 142

143 144

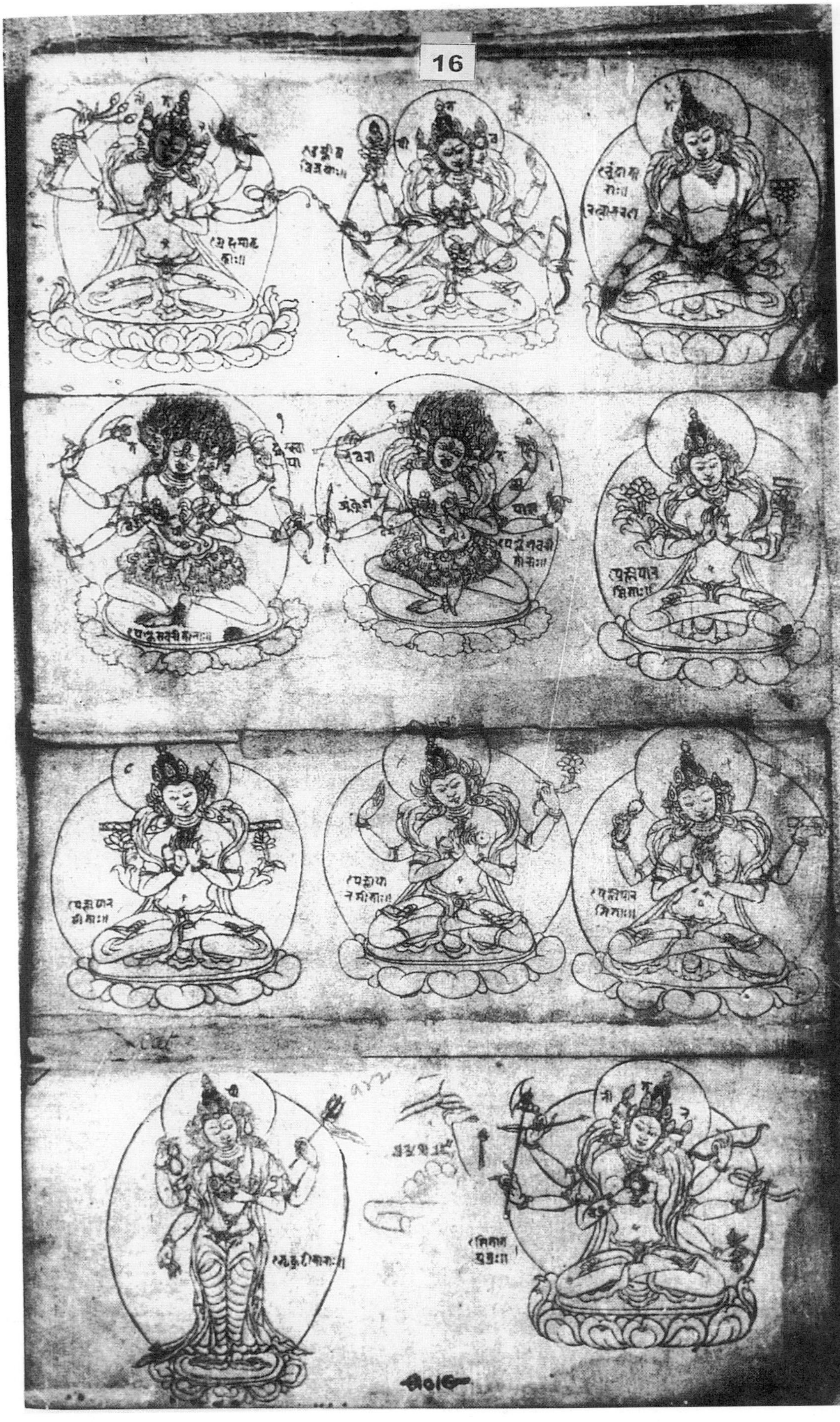

145 146 147

148 149 150

151 152

153 154 155

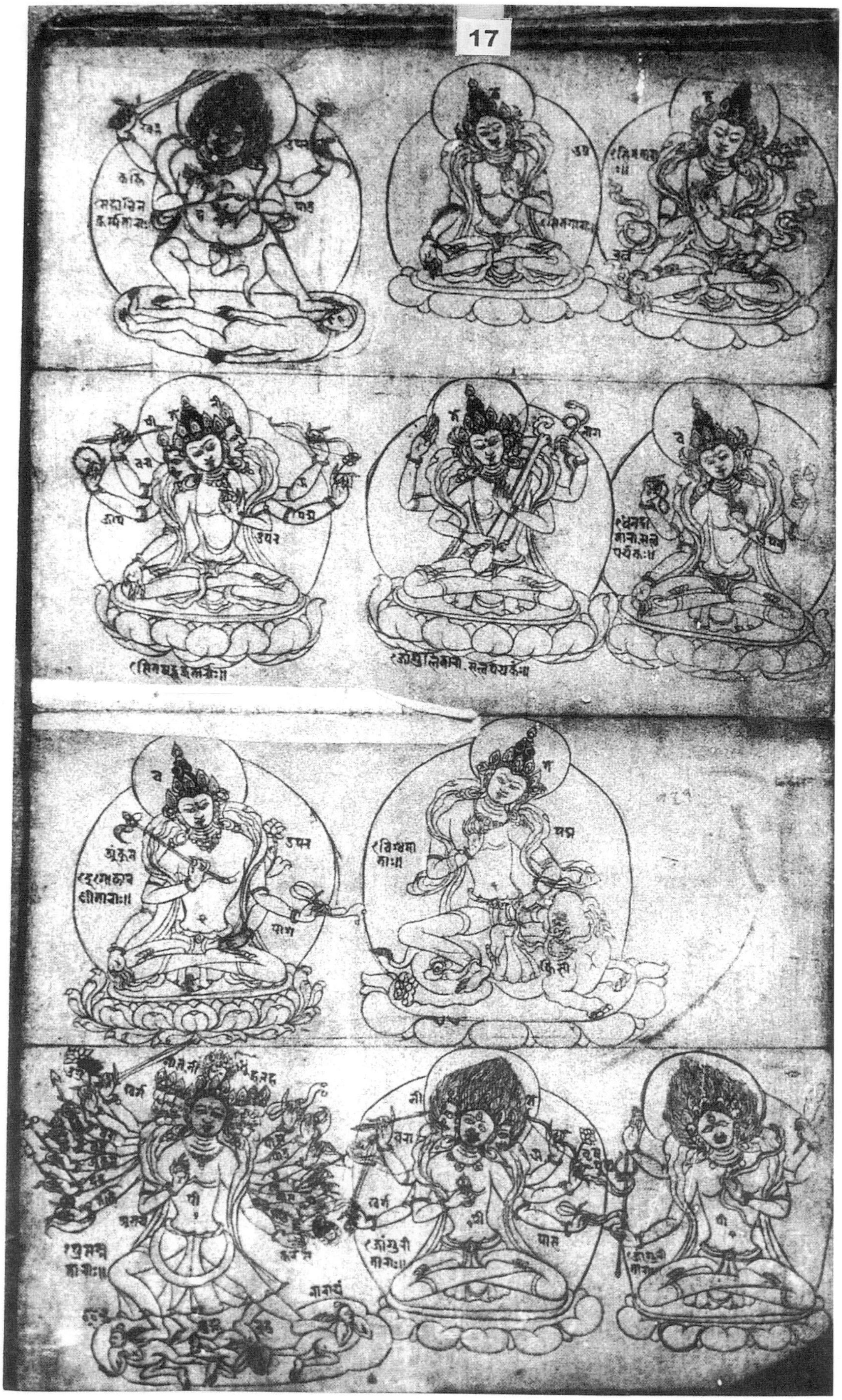

156 157

158 159 160

161 162 163

164 165 166

167 168 169

170 171

Index of Deities' Names in the BDC and LC

Index of Deities' Names in the BDC and LC

Harihariharivāhanodbhava-Lokeśvara BDC 12/LC 82

Hayagrīva BDC 76/LC 110; BDC 79/LC 109; BDC 80/LC 111

Hevajra, *see* Caturbhuja-H., Dvibhuja-H., Hevajra, *caturbhuja*, Hevajra, *ṣaḍbhuja*, Praharaṇamat-H., Ṣaḍbhuja-H.

Hevajra, *caturbhuja* BDC 184

Hevajra, *ṣaḍbhuja* BDC 186

Hevajra-Kurukullā BDC 183

Jambhala BDC 77/LC 112; *see also* Mahāj., Ucchuṣma-J.

Jāṅgulī LC 163

Jāṅgulī Tārā BDC 102/LC 154; BDC 103/LC 155; LC 149

Jñānaḍākinī BDC 140

Jñānadhātu BDC 21/LC 28; BDC 50/LC 17

Jñānakāya-Mañjuśrī BDC 70/LC 100

Kalpokta-Daśabhuja-Mārīcī BDC 153

Kamalabhadra LC 43

Kamaṇḍalu-Lokeśvara BDC 49/LC 16

Khasarpaṇa-Lokeśvara LC 71

Kiṃcidvistara-Tārā BDC 99/LC 166

Krodha-Lokeśvara, *see* Māyājālakrama-Krodha-Lokeśvara

Kr̥ṣṇācala LC 44

Kr̥ṣṇayamāri BDC 174

Kr̥tāñjali BDC 17/LC 24

Kurukullā, *see* Hevajra-Kurukullā

Lokanātha-Lokeśvara BDC 52/LC 75

Lokeśvara, *see* Amoghapāśa-L., Halāhala-L., Harihariharivāhana-L., Harihariharivāhanodbhava-L., Kamaṇḍalu-L., Lokanātha-L., Māyājālakrama-

Krodha-L., Nīlakaṇṭha-L., Pretasaṃtarpita-L., Ṣaḍakṣarī-L., Sugatisaṃdarśana-L., Sukhāvatī-L., Trailokyavaśaṃkara-L., Vajradharma-L., Vajrapadma-L.

Mahā-Amoghasiddhi BDC 118/LC 131

Mahābala BDC 144; BDC 145

Mahācīnakrama-Tārā LC 145

Mahājambhala BDC 82/LC 114

Mahākāla BDC 60/LC 92; BDC 63/LC 91; BDC 66/LC 96

Mahāmantrānusāraṇī, *see* Dharmacakrasamādhi

Mahāmāyūrī BDC 131/LC 8; BDC 137/LC 14

Mahāpratisarā BDC 135/LC 12

Mahārāga-Mañjuśrī BDC 64/LC 90

Mahārājalīlā-Mañjuśrī BDC 8/LC 62

Mahāratnasaṃbhava *nāmasaṃgītisa lhāṅā* BDC 119/LC 132

Mahāsāhasrapramardanī BDC 136/LC 13

Mahāsaṃvara LC 15

Mahāsarasvatī BDC 86/LC 167; LC 122

Mahāsitavatī BDC 138

Mahattarīpa-Tārā BDC 92/LC 158

Mahāvairocana BDC 116/LC 130; BDC 117/LC 133

Mahāvajrasattva BDC 28/LC 35

Maitreya, *see* Maitrī

Maitrī BDC 61/LC 93; BDC 62/LC 94

Maṇidhara, *see* Ṣaḍakṣarī-Maṇidhara

Mañjunātha BDC 24/LC 31

Mañjuśrī BDC 1/LC 56; BDC 46/LC 56; BDC 65/LC 95; BDC 156; LC 63; LC 105; *see also* Ādibuddha-M., Arapacana-M., Jñānakāya-M., Mahārāga-M., Mahārājalīlā-M., Nāmasaṃgītisa lhāṅā M., Prajñājñāna-M., Pupala-M., Siddhaikavīra-M., Vāgīśvara-M., Vajrakhaḍga-M., Vajrānaṅga-M., Vajratīkṣṇa-M.

Mañjuvajra BDC 176

Mantrānusāraṇī BDC 128/LC 5; BDC 134/LC 11; *see also* Dharmacakrasamādhi (Mahāmantrānusāraṇī)

Mārīcī BDC 152; *see also* Aśokakānta-M., Aṣṭabhuja-M., Kalpokta-Daśabhuja-M., Uḍḍiyāna-M.

Māyājālakrama-Krodha-Lokeśvara BDC 53/LC 78

Māyūrī BDC 127/LC 4; LC 160; *see also* Mahāmāyūrī

Nāmasaṃgītisa lhāṅā Mañjuśrī LC 64

Nīlakaṇṭha-Lokeśvara BDC 9/LC 77

Nṛtyanātha BDC 51/LC 19

Padmadhara, *see* Ṣaḍakṣarī-Padmadhara

Padmanṛtyeśvara BDC 57/LC 87; LC 88

Padmanarteśvara, *see* Padmanṛtyeśvara

Parṇaśavarī Tārā BDC 107/LC 137; BDC 108/LC 138

Piṇḍapātra BDC 37/LC 47

Praharaṇamat-Hevajra BDC 180

Prajñājñāna-Mañjuśrī BDC 69/LC 99

Prajñāpāramitā BDC 39/LC 51; BDC 40/LC 49; BDC 41/LC 52; BDC 44/LC 53; BDC 45/LC 54; BDC 109/LC 139; BDC 110/LC 140; BDC 112/LC 142; LC 50; *see also* Tridaṇḍa (= Prajñāpāramitā)

Prasanna-Tārā BDC 101/LC 153

Pratisarā BDC 124/LC 2; BDC 130/LC 7; *see also* Mahāpratisarā

Pratyaṅgirā BDC 90/LC 171

Pretasaṃtarpita-Lokeśvara BDC 56/LC 80

Pupala LC 46

Pupala-Mañjuśrī BDC 36

Raktāryāvalokiteśvara LC 76

Ratna/Rava___(?) LC 45

Ratnasaṃbhava, *see* Mahāratnasaṃbhava *nāmasaṃgītisa lhāṅā*

Śrī-Yogāmbara BDC 173

Sugatisaṃdarśana-Lokeśvara BDC 54/LC 79

Sukhāvatī-Lokeśvara BDC 59/LC 85

Tārā, *see* Āryat., Aśoka-T., Bhadrāsana-Vaśyādhikāra-T., Bhṛkuṭī T., Cundā T., Daṃva-T., Dhanada-T., Durgottāriṇī T., Grahamātṛkā T., Jāṅgulī T., Kiṃcidvistara-T., Mahācīnakrama-T., Mahattarīpa-T., Parṇaśavarī T., Prasanna-T., Sita-Ṣaḍbhuja-T., Sita-T., Sragdharā T., Uṣṇīṣavijayā T., Vajrat., Varada-T., Vidyujjvālākarālī nāmaikajaṭā-T.

Tiḍada, *see* Tridaṇḍa

Trailokyavaśaṃkara-Lokeśvara LC 74

Tridaṇḍa (= Prajñāpāramitā) BDC 38/LC 48

Ucchuṣma-Jambhala BDC 81/LC 113

Uḍḍiyāna-Mārīcī BDC 150; BDC 151

Ūrdhvapāda-Vajrayoginī BDC 166

Uṣṇīṣa BDC 19/LC 25

Uṣṇīṣavijayā LC 135

Uṣṇīṣavijayā Tārā BDC 105

Vāgīśvara, *see* Dharmaśaṅkha-Dharmadhātu-V.

Vāgīśvara-Mañjuśrī BDC 71/LC 101

Vairocana, *see* Mahāvairocana

Vajracarcikā LC 123

Vajradharma-Lokeśvara LC 67

Vajradhāteśvarī BDC 89/LC 170

Vajradhātu BDC 23/LC 30

Vajradhātu(samādhi) BDC 121/LC 129

Vajradhātvīśvarī, *see* Vajradhāteśvarī

Vajraghoṇā BDC 163

Vajrahūtaka BDC 16/LC 22

Vajrajvālānalārka BDC 75/LC 108

Vajrakhaḍga-Mañjuśrī BDC 68/LC 98

Vajrāmṛta Amṛtakuṇḍalī, *see* Caturtha-Vajrāmṛta Amṛtakuṇḍalī

Vajrānaṅga-Mañjuśrī BDC 4/LC 58; BDC 5/LC 59

Vajrapāṇi BDC 143

Vajrarāga-Mañjuśrī LC 60

Vajrasattva, *see* Mahāv., Saṃpuṭa-ukta-V.

Vajraśāradā BDC 87/LC 168

Vajrasarasvatī BDC 88/LC 169

Vajraśṛṅkhalā LC 119; LC 120

Vajratārā BDC 98/LC 165; BDC 141

Vajratīkṣṇa-Mañjuśrī BDC 67/LC 97; BDC 74/LC 104

Vajravārāhī BDC 169; BDC 170

Vajravīṇā-Sarasvatī LC 121

Vajrayoginī BDC 168; *see also* Ādiv., Ūrdhvapāda-V., Vajraghoṇā, Vajravārāhī, Vidyādharī V.

Varada-Tārā BDC 93/LC 159

Vasudhārā BDC 83/LC 115; BDC 84/LC 116; BDC 85/LC 127

Vaśyādhikāra-Tārā, *see* Bhadrāsana-Vaśyādhikāra-Tārā

Vidyādharī Vajrayoginī BDC 167

Vidyujjvālākarālī nāmaikajaṭā-Tārā BDC 158

Vighnāntaka BDC 146; BDC 147

Viṣṇukānta BDC 15/LC 23

Viśvahara BDC 25/LC 32

Viśvamātā BDC 100/LC 152

Vṛdāyaka BDC 13/LC 20

Yamadaṇḍa BDC 18/LC 26

Yamāśvavajra BDC 78/LC 107

Yogāmbara BDC 172; *see also* Śrī-Yogāmbara